RENAISSANCE

VOLUME 2

Books and Libraries — Constantinople

GROLIER
EDUCATIONAL

Published by Grolier Educational
Sherman Turnpike
Danbury, Connecticut 06816

© 2002 Brown Partworks Limited

Set ISBN 0-7172-5673-1
Volume 2 ISBN 0-7172-5664-2

Library of Congress Cataloging-in-Publication Data

Renaissance.
    p. cm.
Summary: Chronicles the cultural and artistic flowering
known as the Renaissance that flourished in Europe and
in other parts of the world from approximately 1375 to
1575 A.D.
Includes index.
Contents: v. 1. Africa–Bologna — v. 2. Books and libraries–
Constantinople — v. 3. Copernicus–Exploration — v. 4.
Eyck–Government — v. 5. Guilds and crafts–Landscape
painting — v. 6. Language–Merchants — v. 7. Michelangelo–
Palaces and villas — v. 8. Palestrina–Reformation — v. 9.
Religious dissent–Tapestry — v. 10. Technology–Zwingli.
  ISBN 0-7172-5673-1 (set : alk. paper)
  1. Renaissance—Juvenile literature. [1. Renaissance.]
I. Grolier Educational (Firm)
  CB361 .R367 2002
  940.2'1—dc21
                                2002002477

For information address the publisher:
Grolier Educational, Sherman Turnpike,
Danbury, Connecticut 06816

FOR BROWN PARTWORKS

Project Editor: Shona Grimbly
Deputy Editor: Rachel Bean
Text Editor: Chris King
Designer: Sarah Williams
Picture Research: Veneta Bullen
Maps: Colin Woodman
Design Manager: Lynne Ross
Production: Matt Weyland
Managing Editor: Tim Cooke
Consultant: Stephen A. McKnight
                       University of Florida

Printed and bound in Singapore

ABOUT THIS BOOK

This is one of a set of 10 books that tells the story of the Renaissance—a time of discovery and change in the world. It was during this period—roughly from 1375 to 1575—that adventurous mariners from Europe sailed the vast oceans in tiny ships and found the Americas and new sea routes to the Spice Islands of the East. The influx of gold and silver from the New World and the increase in trade made many merchants and traders in Europe extremely rich. They spent some of their wealth on luxury goods like paintings and gold and silver items for their homes, and this created a new demand for the work of artists of all kinds. Europe experienced a cultural flowering as great artists like Leonardo da Vinci, Michelangelo, and Raphael produced masterpieces that have never been surpassed.

At the same time, scholars were rediscovering the works of the ancient Greek and Roman writers, and this led to a new way of looking at the world based on observation and the importance of the individual. This humanism, together with other new ideas, spread more rapidly than ever before thanks to the development of printing with movable type.

There was upheaval in the church too. Thinkers such as Erasmus and Luther began to question the teachings of the established church, and this eventually led to a breakaway from the Catholic church and the setting up of Protestant churches—an event called the Reformation.

The set focuses on Europe, but it also looks at how societies in other parts of the world such as Africa, China, India, and the Americas were developing, and the ways in which the Islamic and Christian worlds interacted.

The entries in this set are arranged alphabetically and are illustrated with paintings, photographs, drawings, and maps, many from the Renaissance period. Each entry ends with a list of cross-references to other entries in the set, and at the end of each book there is a timeline to help you relate events to one another in time.

There is also a useful "Further Reading" list that includes websites, a glossary of special terms, and an index covering the whole set.

Contents

VOLUME 2

Books and Libraries

Books and libraries were crucial to the intellectual life that characterized the Renaissance. Scholars created a demand for copies of ancient Greek and Roman texts, and a growing number of educated people purchased religious books, practical guides, and popular literature.

Below: A page from an early 15th-century French book that was created entirely by hand—from the lettering to the illustration and the decorations around the page border.

In the Middle Ages learning and book production had been confined to monasteries. Monks copied books by hand

and illustrated them; most books were kept in monastery libraries or were owned by the very rich. During the 14th and 15th centuries, however, literacy among lay (nonchurch) people increased dramatically, and more people began to own and collect books. Prayer books and books about saints' lives and the miracles of the Virgin Mary were popular, and educated people also owned books about hunting, falconry, herbal cures, and manners, as well as popular romances and travel books.

To supply this new demand, bookstores were established in all major European cities, and for the first time books were copied outside of monasteries and church control. A typical bookstore opened onto the street and had a scriptorium behind, where scribes made new copies of books and manuscripts.

The books produced in these stores were usually unillustrated, work-a-day objects, made quickly and cheaply to supply popular demand. Lavishly illustrated books were created specially for rich patrons, but they were extremely expensive and took a long time to make.

THE PRINTING REVOLUTION

Book production was revolutionized by the printing process developed in about 1455 by the German Johannes Gutenberg (about 1390–1468). The new process enabled multiple copies of pages to be produced quickly and cheaply, making the spread of information and ideas quicker, easier, and cheaper than ever before. By the 1470s there were printing presses throughout Europe, mostly at universities. By the 1550s almost all books were produced this way.

Gutenberg's process used movable type, which consisted of separate metal blocks, each cast with a letter, number, or punctuation mark. These blocks were arranged in rows between metal rods to create a page of text. They were placed on the flat surface (bed) of a press, covered with ink, and a sheet of paper was pressed onto them.

Printers usually sold printed pages loose, and purchasers paid to have them bound (fastened together and covered) into books afterward. Covers were made from wooden boards, which for wealthy purchasers might be covered with expensive materials such as silk, velvet, or leather, and decorated with gold designs. If people had large collections of books, they usually had them bound to match each other in what are known as library bindings.

Because it cost a great deal to make type, purchase a press, and buy paper, printers were often financed by wealthy backers such as merchants or bankers. It was important that the books produced sold well. Gutenberg printed the Bible, the most popular book ever. William Caxton (about 1422–1491), the first man to set up a printing press in England, published very successful editions of popular literature, such as a translation of the French *Romance of Troy* and Chaucer's *The Canterbury Tales*. Some cities, such as Venice, became important centers of printing.

LIBRARIES SET UP

From the 14th century educated kings, princes, and lords began to amass private libraries to enhance their status as learned men and patrons of the arts. They appointed special advisers to select and purchase their books, which were lavishly illustrated and expensively

bound. Great libraries were put together by Duke Philip the Good of Burgundy, kings Louis IX and Charles V of France, Cosimo and Lorenzo de Medici in Italy, Diane de Poitiers, the mistress of King Henry II of France, King Matthias I of Hungary, King Philip II of Spain, and kings Henry VII and VIII of England. Scholars and writers such as Petrarch and Boccaccio also collected books.

During the Reformation, when the Protestant church broke away from the Roman Catholic church, many of the monasteries of northern Europe were were destroyed. Along with the monasteries, their libraries were also destroyed, but some of the books were saved and found their way into the hands of private collectors. Later these books were to form the backbone of great public collections such as the British Library in London and the Bodleian Library at Oxford University.

In Germany the religious reformer Martin Luther instructed all German towns to set up a public library, and many books from the monasteries found their way into these collections. Some of the great princely libraries were also opened to the public, notably those of Cosimo de Medici and Lorenzo de Medici in Florence.

Above: The reading room in the Laurentian Library in Florence. The library was built in the 16th century, and the basis of its collection came from the private library of Cosimo de Medici, amassed in the 15th century.

SEE ALSO

♦ Chaucer
♦ Christine de Pisan
♦ Dante
♦ Education
♦ Literacy
♦ Literature
♦ Luther
♦ Petrarch
♦ Printing
♦ Universities

Borgia Family

The Borgia family originated in Spain, but several of its members followed Cardinal Alfonso Borgia to Rome after he became Pope Calixtus III in 1455. The family became prominent in the political affairs of Renaissance Italy, but also gained an infamous reputation for corruption and violence.

Alfonso Borgia (1378–1458) was old and ill when he became pope and reigned for only three years. He was pious and charitable, but he became unpopular in Italy for the favors and lucrative jobs he gave to his relatives and other Spaniards.

Among those who benefited in this way was Alfonso's nephew Rodrigo Borgia (1431–1503), who was given a string of positions in the church. Rodrigo managed to build up a considerable fortune through these posts. Eventually, he became pope as Alexander VI in 1492. He gained the office partly by bribing other cardinals to vote for him.

FAMILY MATTERS

Alexander was a skillful administrator and had an interest in the arts, but he devoted much of his time to increasing his family's wealth and power. He often created scandal and had several illegitimate children, among them his son Cesare (1475–1507) and his daughter Lucrezia (1480–1519). Alexander made many enemies, and it was rumored that his death was the result of poisoning, although the official cause was malaria.

Cesare was given various church posts by his father and became a cardinal when he was only 18. However, he resigned his church positions after the murder of his brother Juan in 1497, taking over his position as commander of the papal army. Many people believed Cesare to be responsible for his brother's death, although his involvement was never proven.

THE PURSUIT OF POWER

Encouraged by Alexander, Cesare conquered various cities in central Italy, bringing their territories under the control of the papacy. In the course of

Above: The Borgia coat of arms, which is emblazoned on a ceiling in their apartments in the Vatican Palace, Rome. There were two Borgia popes— Calixtus III and Alexander VI.

these campaigns he gained a reputation for utter ruthlessness against anyone who stood in his way. During this period Cesare employed the artist Leonardo da Vinci for a time as a military engineer.

The death of his father in 1503 signaled the end of Cesare's power.

Cesare Borgia continues to capture the imagination as one of the most intriguing figures of the Renaissance

---

The new pope, Julius II (pope 1503–1513), was an enemy of the Borgias and had Cesare arrested and imprisoned in Spain. He escaped in 1506, but was killed the following year while serving in the army of his brother-in-law, the king of Navarre.

Although he was hated by many for his cruelty and treachery, Cesare also had attractive qualities, since he was handsome, brave, intelligent, and cultivated. Because of this striking mixture of good and bad features he has continued to capture the imagination as one of the most intriguing figures of the Renaissance.

DUTIFUL DAUGHTER

In her early years Lucrezia Borgia was used as a pawn in the political maneuverings of her father and brother. By the age of 22 she had been married three times to cement various alliances. Her first marriage ended in divorce, while her second husband was murdered on Cesare's orders in 1500.

Two years later Lucretia was married for the third and final time to Alfonso d'Este, who became duke of

Ferrara in 1505. As duchess of Ferrara, the beautiful and intelligent Lucrezia presided over a cultured court and became known for her charitable works. She continued to be the subject of many malicious stories, however. She was widely believed to have committed incest with both her father and her brother, although these rumors may have been put about by her family's many enemies.

It was a later-born member of the family who helped repair its damaged reputation. One of the great-grandsons of Alexander VI, Francis Borgia (1510–1572), was a devout and energetic priest. Such was Francis' piety that in 1671 he was declared a saint.

SEE ALSO

♦ Alexander VI
♦ Italy
♦ Julius II
♦ Papacy
♦ Papal States

Below: A portrait of Cesare Borgia, the illegitimate son of Pope Alexander VI. Cesare was feared as a ruthlessly cruel politician and military leader.

Bosch

Hieronymus Bosch (about 1450–1516) painted some of the best-known and most extraordinary pictures in the history of art. Some are nightmarish visions of demons and strange creatures that are part-human and part-animal. Others offer a wholly original interpretation of themes that obsessed people of his time, such as the terrible punishments that awaited sinners.

Little is known about Bosch or the circumstances in which he created his pictures. He appears to have spent all his life in 's-Hertogenbosch (from which he took his name), a prosperous Dutch city near the present-day Belgian border. It was not a major artistic center, and Bosch's paintings are quite unlike the serene, courtly pictures produced in Bruges, Brussels, and Antwerp. Despite this, he enjoyed the support of powerful patrons, and Philip II of Spain collected his work.

HEAVEN AND HELL

Bosch's largest and most famous painting is *The Garden of Earthly Delights* (about 1500–1510). It is typical of his work in its mass of detail, polished finish, and complex imagery, which is probably based on medieval folklore and verbal puns (word plays). The picture consists of three panels hinged together (a format known as a triptych) and shows how the pursuit of pleasure can lead to sin.

The left-hand panel of Bosch's masterpiece shows God with Adam and Eve in the Garden of Eden. It is

Left: The right-hand panel of Bosch's triptych (three-part painting) entitled The Garden of Earthly Delights, *which was painted between 1500 and 1510. It shows sinners being punished in hell and all manner of nightmarish creatures and weird inventions.*

a landscape of delicate greens and pinks populated by exotic plants and animals. The alluring beauty of this scene spills over into the central panel, where lots of naked men and women are engaged in dancing, feasting, and lovemaking. Nature has gone awry, however—fruits, fish, and birds are as big as men, and strange contraptions stand in the lake.

Even so, these weird distortions are nothing compared to the nightmarish vision of hell in the third panel. One of Bosch's most haunting inventions dominates the scene: a melancholy "tree man" inside whose broken body is a tavern. Behind him is a terrible weapon made from a gigantic knife mounted between a pair of ears, while all around people are tormented by demons and devoured by monsters.

SEE ALSO

♦ Flemish Painting

Botany

Above: A woodcut illustration from a book of botanical studies published in 1542 by the German botanist Leonhard Fuchs.

Botany is the branch of science dealing with plants. It involves the study of their structure, properties, and the ways they can be classified (arranged into groups of related plants). Plants were important during the Renaissance period because people used them to make herbal medicines, but detailed botanical studies were not carried out until after 1500.

During the Middle Ages and the early Renaissance knowledge about plants was based on ancient Greek texts. The most important of these early studies was by Theophrastus (371–287 B.C.). However, Theophrastus's work had been largely forgotten by the 14th century. By then most knowledge about plants was based on texts by the Greek physician (doctor) Dioscorides (about 40–90 A.D.), who only described plants used for medicines.

Based on Dioscorides' example, medieval and Renaissance botany centered on herbals. Herbals were books that listed and described plants according to their medicinal properties. They did not attempt to classify plants according to any theoretical framework. Natural philosophers (early scientists) copied and commented on classical (ancient Greek and Roman) works rather than actually examining plants. However, the local plants described by Dioscorides often differed from those growing outside Greece, which led to confusion.

In the late 15th century exploration of the Americas and trade stimulated the science of botany. People began to realize that the ancient Greek texts were inaccurate and excluded plants growing elsewhere in Europe and farther afield. Botanists like the German physician Otto Brunfels (1488–1534) and his countryman Leonhard Fuchs (1501–1566) examined the local plants of their country and recorded them with accurate drawings and descriptions. So did the Italian physician and botanist Luca Ghini (1490–1566), who introduced the technique of drying plants between sheets of paper and mounting them for further study.

Botanists also began to study non-medicinal plants. Botanical gardens (containing collections of plants for studying) were founded, starting with those at the Italian universities of Pisa (1543) and Padua (1545).

EARLY CLASSIFICATION SYSTEMS

Many new plants were discovered and described, but there was still no classification system for categorizing them by species. In the early 16th century the Swiss botanist and physician Conrad Gesner (1516–1565) noted that flowers and fruits could be used as a basis for classification. Then in 1583 the Italian botanist Andrea Cesalpino (1519–1603) published a 16-volume study of plants, describing more than 1,500 plants and classifying them according to their fruits. This book is considered the first textbook of botany. However, it was not until the 18th century that the Swede Carolus Linnaeus defined the different parts of plants and established the system of classification used today.

Botticelli

The great Italian artist Sandro Botticelli (about 1444–1510) created what have become some of the best-known paintings of the Renaissance: *The Birth of Venus* and *Primavera* ("Spring"). They are the first important Renaissance pictures based on classical (ancient Greek and Roman) myths. They also show the graceful style that made Botticelli the most popular painter in Florence.

Botticelli was born in Florence and spent almost all his life there. He trained in the workshop of Filippo Lippi (about 1406–1469), one of the leading Florentine painters of the time. Lippi's delicate, decorative style had a great influence on the young Botticelli. By 1470 Botticelli was established as an independent artist with his own workshop. He rapidly made a name for himself, and by about 1480 he was the most sought-after painter in Florence.

Botticelli's busy workshop produced pictures for the city's most important churches, for the civic authorities, and for some of Florence's richest and most powerful families, including the Medici. His reputation also spread beyond Florence. In 1481 Pope Sixtus IV commissioned Botticelli—along with other leading painters of the time—to produce wall paintings in the Sistine Chapel in Rome.

ARTISTIC THEMES

Most of Botticelli's paintings were of religious subjects. *The Madonna of the Magnificat*, painted in about 1480, is typical of these works. It shows Mary writing in a book, with the infant Jesus sitting on her lap. Around them are five angels, two of whom are placing a delicate gold crown on Mary's head. The figures are graceful and have sweet faces. Fine lines of gold are used to highlight their curling locks of hair and the patterns edging their delicately painted clothes. A landscape with a

---

By about 1480 Botticelli was the most sought-after painter in Florence

---

river and rolling hills is glimpsed in the background. The painting is round; pictures this shape are called *tondi* (from the Latin *rotundus*, meaning "round") and became very popular in the Renaissance.

Although Botticelli mainly chose religious themes, he also painted a number of outstanding secular (non-religious) portraits, including *Portrait of a Young Man Holding a Medal* (about 1475). Again, a softly painted landscape

Above: Botticelli's picture Primavera *("Spring"), painted in about 1477. He depicted spring as a beautiful goddess (center) in a flower-filled meadow. She is accompanied by Flora (right), goddess of flowers, who is shown wearing a flowery dress, and three elegant, dancing figures called the Three Graces (left).*

forms the background, and the young man's elegant face appears smooth, with crisply outlined features.

In addition to paintings Botticelli created some of the finest drawings of the Renaissance, including a series of illustrations to Dante's epic poem *The Divine Comedy*.

MYTHOLOGICAL SUBJECTS

However, it is Botticelli's mythological scenes that are most famous. He was the first artist since the days of ancient Rome to paint subjects from classical myths in such a grand and serious way. *Primavera* (about 1477) and *The Birth of Venus* (about 1485, see box) were both produced for Lorenzo di Pierfrancesco de Medici, a wealthy merchant. The paintings show the new popularity of classical myths in the Renaissance, when they were widely read by educated people. Myths were valued as appealing stories and were also given complex interpretations by some scholars who believed that they expressed philosophical truths of the ancient world.

Lorenzo was an educated man, and it is likely that he or his scholarly friends gave Botticelli precise instructions on how the subjects should be depicted.

FALL FROM FAVOR

In the 1490s Botticelli's career went into decline. It was a time of political unrest in Florence, when the Medici were expelled from the city, and Girolamo Savonarola, a friar who preached fervently against sinfulness and luxury, became head of a puritanical government. Botticelli's later paintings appear to show the influence of Savonarola's teachings. The pictures lack the grace of Botticelli's earlier work and are more emotionally charged.

It is also likely that Botticelli's graceful style of painting seemed old-fashioned, particularly after Leonardo da Vinci returned to the city in 1500 after a long period in Milan. By the time of his death Botticelli was virtually forgotten, and it was not until the 19th century that his reputation underwent a great revival.

SEE ALSO
- Artists' Workshops
- Boccaccio
- Dante
- Landscape Painting
- Mythological Art
- Painting
- Savonarola

THE BIRTH OF VENUS

The Birth of Venus is one of Botticelli's most famous pictures. According to Greek myth, Venus was born in the sea and was washed ashore on a giant scallop shell, blown by the winds. Her birth was seen as symbolizing the entry of beauty into the world. It is likely that scholars told Botticelli what was known about the way classical artists had shown the scene and how he should portray the subject. On the left is Zephyr, god of the west wind, and Aurora, goddess of dawn. Zephyr puffs out his cheeks and blows Venus ashore, showering her with roses. The goddess Flora stands to the right, holding out a billowing cloak for Venus. The figures are painted with grace, their smooth white skin, delicate swirling clothes, and elegant poses creating a picture of great harmony and beauty.

Above: Botticelli's **The Birth of Venus** *(about 1485), which was inspired by classical art and literature.*

Bramante

Donato Bramante (about 1444–1514) was the greatest Italian architect of his time. In combining aspects of classical (ancient Greek and Roman) architecture with Renaissance ideas about harmony, he created some of the most influential buildings of the period. His small church in Rome known as the Tempietto is the best-known example of his work.

Bramante was born near Urbino and spent most of his career in Milan, working as a painter and architect for the powerful Sforza family who ruled the city. He was friendly with Leonardo da Vinci, who also worked for the Sforzas. In 1499 the French invasion of northern Italy and the overthrow of the Sforzas forced Bramante to flee south to Rome. It was there that he created his most important buildings.

THE TEMPIETTO

Soon after he arrived in Rome, Bramante began work on the tiny church known as the Tempietto (little temple), built on the spot where Saint Peter was thought to have been martyred.

The Tempietto's design is based on a circle. The church is a cylinder surrounded by columns and topped by a dome. Renaissance scholars considered the circle to be the perfect shape, and architects often tried to use it in their designs. It was especially appropriate for the Tempietto because early Christians had built round churches to commemorate holy people or places. Bramante successfully combined the circular shape with classical elements such as columns, and his design influenced generations of architects.

In 1506 Bramante began work on the most important architectural project of the day—the rebuilding of the great church of Saint Peter's. The original Saint Peter's was well over a thousand years old and in a poor state of repair. Pope Julius II (pope 1503–1513) decided to demolish it and commissioned Bramante to build a new church.

Bramante designed a huge dome, as big as the one covering the Pantheon. Although he died before it could be built, the massive supports designed by Bramante determined the proportions of the building when it was eventually completed a century later.

Above: Bramante's Tempietto in Rome, designed in about 1502. This tiny church was admired by Renaissance architects, who thought it equaled the achievements of the classical world.

SEE ALSO

♦ Architecture
♦ Classicism
♦ Saint Peter's, Rome

Right: Bronzino's Portrait of Eleonora of Toledo (Cosimo de Medici's wife), painted in 1545. Bronzino shows Eleonora in a sumptuous dress with one of her sons. He painted them with smooth, white skin and made Eleonora's hands long and thin to enhance the feeling of elegance and sophistication.

Bronzino

A gnolo Bronzino (1503–1572) was the leading artist in Florence in the mid-16th century. He was a personal favorite of Duke Cosimo de Medici, the ruler of the city, and he spent much of his career working for him. Bronzino's portraits of Cosimo's family and courtiers reflect the sophisticated world in which they lived, and it is these pictures for which he is best known.

Bronzino was born just outside Florence and trained in the workshop of Jacopo Pontormo (1494–1557). Pontormo treated him like a son, and Bronzino continued to work with him long after his apprenticeship ended. They painted in a similar style, and it is often difficult to tell their work apart.

Both artists worked in a refined style known as mannerism that reflected the sophisticated, courtly lifestyle of their patrons. The surfaces of their paintings appear smooth and highly polished—the skin often looks like porcelain—and figures and objects are painted with clear outlines and strong contrasts of light and shade. Their larger pictures are packed with figures in complicated poses that are variations on classical (ancient Greek and Roman) and Renaissance works of art, particularly those of Michelangelo. Pontormo and Bronzino elongated their figures to make them look elegant and gave them sweet, idealized faces.

DUKE COSIMO'S FAVORITE

Bronzino began working for Duke Cosimo de Medici in 1539, and he was at his busiest during the 1540s. In that decade he painted numerous portraits of Cosimo and his family. One of the most famous shows Cosimo's wife Eleonora of Toledo with one of their sons (either Francesco or Giovanni). Bronzino also produced frescoes (wall paintings) and tapestry designs to decorate the Palazzo Vecchio, Cosimo's main residence in Florence.

Another well-known picture by Bronzino that was painted in the 1540s is *The Allegory of Love*. It shows Venus, goddess of love, and her son Cupid embracing, surrounded by figures and objects that symbolize love and the passage of time. The symbols drew on contemporary scholarly thought and were intended to appeal to cultivated tastes, although the painting's main appeal is its sensuality.

In his later years Bronzino devoted more of his time to religious paintings. He was also involved in running Florence's Academy of Design, which was the first art academy in Europe.

SEE ALSO
♦ Mannerism
♦ Painting

Bruegel, Pieter the Elder

Above: **Hunters in the Snow,** *painted by Bruegel in 1565. It shows a wintry landscape and is one of a series of pictures by Bruegel depicting different times of the year.*

Pieter Bruegel (about 1525–1569) was one of the greatest northern European painters of the 16th century. He is best known for his detailed and often humorous depictions of life in the region's villages and countryside. He painted colorful, bustling scenes full of people engaged in everyday activities, as well as views of snow-covered landscapes.

Nothing is known about Bruegel's life before 1551, when he became a member of the painters' guild in Antwerp. Soon afterward he traveled to Italy to complete his education, as many artists were beginning to do. He returned to Antwerp in 1555 and then moved to Brussels in 1563.

One of the main characteristics of Bruegel's paintings is the decorative appeal of their colors and shapes. These qualities are beautifully shown in his painting *Children's Games* (1560) in which a broad street is packed full of children playing all sorts of games—rolling hoops, playing leapfrog, and walking on stilts. The shapes of their tiny bending, crouching, and running bodies and the reds and greens of their clothes are as attractive as the detail of their activities.

LANDSCAPES AND PEASANTS

Bruegel also excelled at painting landscapes. Some of his greatest achievements were the landscapes he painted showing different seasons of the year, which were created in the last 10 to 12 years of his life. The best known, *Hunters in the Snow* (1565), shows hunters and their dogs returning wearily home through thick snow. On the outskirts of their village people are skating on frozen ponds. A valley with fields and bare trees spreads into the distance, hemmed in by craggy mountains.

As well as scenes of peasant life, including boisterous dances and wedding feasts, Bruegel painted religious pictures and parables (moralizing stories). He set these subjects in 16th-century villages, as if they were part of everyday life. Although artists often painted parables in this way, it was the first time holy subjects had been treated like this.

Bruegel's paintings were popular with wealthy merchants and aristocrats, and continued to be avidly collected after his death. Other painters carried on his style, particularly his two sons Pieter the Younger (1564–1638) and Jan (1568–1625).

Bruges

In the 14th and 15th centuries the city of Bruges was one of the busiest and most prosperous ports in Europe. It was located in the region of Flanders—which covered parts of present-day France, Belgium, and the Netherlands—and was positioned at the junction of several trade routes. The city had strong commercial links with England, France, Germany, and Italy. It was also an important industrial center, particularly for cloth and textile manufacture. Traders from all over Europe traveled to Bruges to do business there.

In 1301, when the French queen Jeanne of Navarre visited Bruges, she commented that some merchants' wives were so magnificently dressed that they looked like queens themselves. The

Left: The court building in Bruges, which was built in the 1530s. It is one of the many fine buildings constructed in the Renaissance, when Bruges was one of Europe's most prosperous cities.

> *Among the artists who lived in Bruges was Jan van Eyck, the leading Flemish painter of the 15th century*

city's wealth and status were not only reflected in the finery of its citizens, however; they were also expressed in the magnifence of its architecture. The many fine buildings dating from the Renaissance period include the lavishly decorated town hall and the market hall, the tower of which soared 260 ft (80m) into the sky.

Bruges was a place where the visual arts flourished. Many artists worked there, including Jan van Eyck (about 1395–1441), the leading Flemish painter of the 15th century. Van Eyck moved to Bruges in about 1430 and lived there until his death. His most famous portrait shows one of the city's wealthy couples—the Italian merchant Giovanni Arnolfini and his wife Giovanna Cenami, painted for their marriage.

DECLINE IN IMPORTANCE

Bruges began to lose its commercial importance in the 15th century because the river connecting it with the North Sea became blocked by mud, restricting the passage of trading ships. By 1500 Antwerp had replaced it as the region's leading port. However, Bruges kept its status as a cultural center until the later years of the 16th century, when it was devastated by the religious and political conflict that took place in Flanders at that time. Since then, the region around Bruges has often been the scene of warfare; despite this, many of its Renaissance buildings still survive.

SEE ALSO
- Eyck, Jan van
- Flemish Painting
- Netherlands
- Tapestry
- Textiles

Brunelleschi

The architect Filippo Brunelleschi (1377–1446) was one of a group of outstanding artists who made Florence the center of the Renaissance at the beginning of the 15th century. Brunelleschi was the first architect to study how ancient Roman buildings were constructed and to revive the use of classical elements in an ordered way. He combined these elements with a new concern for harmony and in so doing influenced the course of Renaissance architecture.

Brunelleschi was born in Florence and trained both as a goldsmith and as a sculptor. In 1401 to 1402 he entered a prestigious competition to design a set of decorated bronze doors for the baptistery (the place where baptisms are carried out) of Florence Cathedral. The competition was won by the sculptor Lorenzo Ghiberti. Soon afterward Brunelleschi began to study architecture and probably made the first of several visits to Rome to examine the city's Roman antiquities.

In 1418 Brunelleschi was engaged on the most important architectural project of his day, which was the design of the dome for Florence Cathedral. Work on the cathedral had begun in 1294, but none of the masons (builders) had been able to work out how to build the dome. They had constructed an octagonal (eight-sided) base that measured 138 ft (42m) across, but they could get no further. The problem was that medieval building techniques required the use of a massive wooden framework called centering to support the dome as it was being constructed. There were no timbers large enough for the job; and even if there had been, they would have collapsed under their own weight before a single stone was laid on top of them.

BRUNELLESCHI'S SOLUTION

Brunelleschi's solution was to design a dome that did not need to be supported by centering while it was being constructed; it also had to be light enough not to crush the existing walls. His dome is pointed, with a skeleton of eight vertical, arched ribs that rise from the octagonal base; horizontal ribs tie the vertical ribs together. The dome is topped by a feature known as a

Below: The dome of Florence Cathedral, which was designed by Brunelleschi between about 1418 and 1436. Brunelleschi was influenced by Roman buildings, and the dome is considered to be the first building of the Renaissance.

BRUNELLESCHI AND PERSPECTIVE

Although Brunelleschi is best known for his architecture, he also developed linear perspective, a mathematical system that enables artists to create the illusion of space in their pictures. He painted two pictures of streets to demonstrate his system, but neither survives. The painting of the Holy Trinity (about 1425) by his friend Masaccio is the first painting known to be based on Brunelleschi's system. From this time on, perspective had a great effect on Renaissance artists, helping them make their pictures look more lifelike.

lantern that acts as a stopper, anchoring the tops of the ribs.

To make the dome lighter, Brunelleschi designed it as two shells rather than a solid structure. He used brick rather than stone on the top section to reduce the weight further. He also ensured that each layer of stone or brick was bonded (attached) to the layer below in such a way that it supported its own weight, making centering unnecessary—a technique Brunelleschi almost certainly developed from his study of Roman buildings.

OTHER BUILDINGS IN FLORENCE

While he worked on the dome, Brunelleschi designed many other buildings in Florence that had a great influence on the development of Renaissance architecture. The first was the Foundling Hospital (1419–1424), a home for abandoned children. The building is significant because Brunelleschi used elements from ancient Roman architecture in an ordered way, something that set him apart from earlier architects. This ordered approach can be seen in the open gallery (loggia) that runs around the courtyard at the center of the building, with its columns, pilasters (flattened columns), and round arches.

Brunelleschi also designed two churches—San Lorenzo (begun 1419) and Santo Spirito (about 1434)—and a small chapel, the Pazzi Chapel (about 1430), at the Church of Santa Croce. All three use the same ordered and refined elements of classical architecture as the Foundling Hospital. They are characterized by their beautifully carved columns, pilasters, and moldings made from gray stone set against white walls.

The three buildings are also based on shapes that contemporary scholars and mathematicians regarded as perfect—the square and circle. In basing his designs on these shapes, Brunelleschi sought to make his buildings harmonious, so that all the different spaces such as the nave (where the congregation sits), the aisles (that run down either side of the nave), and the chapels around the edge related to each other in size and shape.

Above: The inside of the Pazzi Chapel in the Church of Santa Croce, Florence, designed by Brunelleschi in about 1430. The sense of order and classical detailing are typical of Brunelleschi's work.

SEE ALSO

♦ Architecture
♦ Classicism
♦ Florence
♦ Masaccio
♦ Perspective

Calendars and Clocks

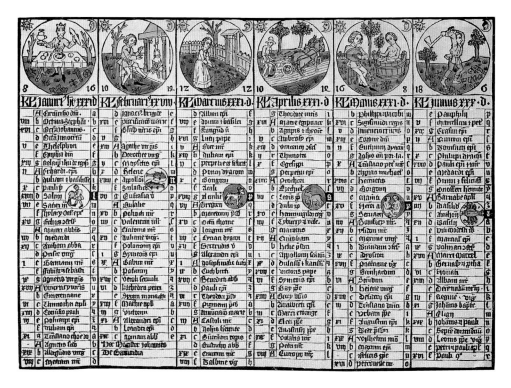

Left: Part of a 15th-century German calendar, showing the months of January to June. Before the calendar was reformed in the 1580s, Europeans followed the Julian calendar, which dated from the first century B.C.

In the Renaissance advances in astronomy and a greater understanding of the annual movements of the earth led to a radical reform of the calendar. At the same time, mechanical clocks gradually became both more common and more accurate.

Up until the 16th century the whole of Europe had followed the Julian calendar, which dated back to Roman times. According to this calendar, the solar year (which we now know is the time it takes the earth to orbit the sun) was 365 days and six hours long. The introduction of a leap year every four years was intended to make sure the calendar corresponded to the seasons.

The solar year, however, is actually made up of 365 days, 5 hours, 48 minutes, and 46 seconds—11 minutes and 14 seconds less than the estimate used to calculate the Julian calendar. This meant that a misalignment between the Julian calendar and the seasons developed over the course of the centuries. As a result religious festivals such as Easter began to fall earlier and earlier in the seasons. Eventually, the Catholic church came under pressure to reform the calendar.

THE GREGORIAN CALENDAR

The task of reforming the Julian calendar was eventually undertaken by Pope Gregory XIII (1502–1585). Aided by the increasingly accurate astronomical observations made by his scientists, he decreed that October 4, 1582, should be followed immediately by October 15. In this way Gregory managed to realign the calendar to the seasons. In order to make sure that the problem did not arise again, he decreed that no century year should be a leap year unless it was exactly divisible by 400, such as the years 1600 and 2000.

The Catholic countries of Europe readjusted their calendars between 1582 and 1583, but the Protestant countries were less willing to comply with an order from the Catholic church. Because of this, many northern European countries did not adopt the calendar until much later. England, for example, did not make the change until 1752.

THE FIRST MECHANICAL CLOCKS

Since ancient times people had used a variety of devices to measure time. The most common were sundials, in which the sun cast a shadow across a clock face. One problem with sundials was that they could not be used at night— or on cloudy days. Other early types of clocks, such as hourglasses and water clocks, were not very accurate.

Slowly, however, mechanical clocks began to appear. These clocks were driven by a system of weights and were first made toward the end of the 13th century. They struck each hour, giving the time "of the clock," or "o'clock." At first, the clocks struck up to 24 times to indicate the hours. However, it was difficult to count 24 separate strokes, so the day was divided into two halves of 12 hours each.

The first public clock to strike the hours was made and put up in Milan in 1335, while the first dial was fitted to a clock in 1344 by Jacopo Dondi of Cluggia. It only had one hand—minute hands did not appear until the end of the 17th century.

The first domestic clocks, which also appeared in the 14th century, were at first simply smaller versions of the large public clocks. Very simple in design, these early domestic clocks stood on a pedestal with an opening to accommodate the weights. They tended to lose or gain as much as half an hour a day, so they required frequent adjustment. In large wealthy households a resident clockmaker was appointed to maintain the clocks.

At the beginning of the 16th century Peter Henlein, a German locksmith, began to make small spring-driven clocks. This revolutionary development meant that timepieces were portable for the first time. These early watches were carried in the hand and were known as "Nuremberg eggs."

From this point onward domestic spring-driven clocks became more common. Despite these changes, however, most ordinary people's sense of time remained inexact, reliant still on the sound of church bells or the position of the sun in the daytime and the cries of watchmen at night.

Left: A weight-driven domestic clock of the early 16th century. Like other early mechanical clocks, it has only one hand (the hour hand), and there is no glass to protect the clock face from dust.

SEE ALSO

♦ Astronomy
♦ Daily Life

Calvin

John Calvin (1509–1564) was one of the most important figures in the development of Protestantism. His writings helped define its central beliefs. Later, his name was given to a major branch of Protestantism—Calvinism.

Born at Noyon in northern France, Calvin was the son of the secretary to the local bishop. Eager for a high church career for his son, John's father sent him to Paris University to train as a theologian (someone who studies religious faith). There Calvin met humanists—scholars who paid particular attention to ancient Greek and Latin texts, especially the Scriptures. Calvin later moved to the University of Orléans to study for a law degree, which he received in 1532. He then returned to Paris, where he continued his study of classical literature.

Calvin had been brought up as a Roman Catholic, but some time during his education he converted to Protestantism. Inspired by the teachings of the German monk and scholar Martin Luther, Protestants rejected the authority of the pope, instead believing that the Scriptures alone should provide the basis of Christian teachings. Protestants

Above: This portrait in oil by a Flemish artist shows Calvin as a young man.

THE DOCTRINE OF PREDESTINATION

One of the central parts of Calvin's system of beliefs was the doctrine of predestination, which is the idea that God determines the fate of a person's soul before his or her birth. The doctrine was not new to Calvin. Many earlier Christian scholars had believed in it; but they had said that while God chose who should go to heaven, the damned were responsible for their own fate because of their sins. Calvin disagreed because of his emphasis on God's absolute power. He argued that there was nothing that a human could do, whether good or evil, to influence God's will. According to this school of thought, God alone decided the fate of each soul. However, Calvin was eager to keep his followers from believing that it made no difference what they did in life since their fate had already been determined. He proclaimed that those who lived a good Christian life should have reasonable confidence that they were among the saved.

believed the Catholic church to be corrupt and were critical of such practices as the selling of indulgences, which allowed people to make amends for their sins simply by giving money to the church. Since 1517, when Luther had first made his challenge to the church, Protestantism had become extremely popular in northern Europe.

FLIGHT TO SWITZERLAND

Calvin fled from France in 1533 when the government clamped down on opposition to the Catholic church. He moved to Basel in Switzerland. There he wrote the work for which he would be most remembered, his *Institutes of the Christian Religion*, which was published in 1536. The *Institutes* eventually defined an important strand of the Protestant religion.

Among the key concepts that the *Institutes* covered was the idea of predestination, which was central to Calvin's beliefs (see box). Another was the idea that work was a Christian duty, and that people can worship God simply by working hard in whatever profession he has chosen for them. This attitude eventually became known as the Protestant work ethic.

In July 1536, on his way to the German city of Strasbourg to become pastor of the French Protestant community there, Calvin passed through the city of Geneva in Switzerland, which had recently become Protestant. The local Protestant leaders persuaded him to stay. Calvin quickly became the dominant leader in the city, although he soon made political enemies who ousted him in 1538. Calvin fled to Strasbourg, where he was married in 1540.

In 1541 Calvin's supporters regained control of Geneva and invited Calvin to return, which he did reluctantly. He spent the rest of his life there. On his return Calvin set about the task of making Geneva a model Christian city. One important step that Calvin made was the division of church officials into four separate groups: pastors, who preached and administered the two sacraments of baptism and holy communion; teachers, who instructed the faithful; elders, who supervised the citizens' conduct; and deacons, who administered poor relief.

In order to make sure that every aspect of life in Geneva conformed to his religious beliefs, Calvin set up a governing body known as a consistory.

Below: In this 16th-century woodcut Luther (left), the pope (center), and Calvin (right) are shown fighting for control of the church.

LUTHER. PABST CALVINUS

Right: This painting shows a Calvinist preacher delivering a sermon in Lyon, France, in 1564. As in other Calvinist churches, men and women sit separately.

It was made up of the nine pastors and 12 elders. The consistory imposed Calvin's strict moral code, which banned pastimes such as gambling and dancing. This extreme form of Protestantism later became known as Puritanism when it spread first to England and then to the Americas.

OPPOSITION TO CALVIN

Although Calvin dominated Geneva after 1541, he faced opposition from many who did not accept his beliefs. Calvin was not tolerant of these opponents. Some were condemned to death for heresy or treason. The most notorious case involved Michael Servetus, an unorthodox Spanish theologian who came to Geneva in 1553 to debate with Calvin. He was quickly arrested, convicted of heresy, and burned at the stake.

Calvin was determined to reform the entire Christian church, and to do this, he founded the Geneva Academy in 1559. Later known as the University of Geneva, it trained pastors to send across Europe. By the time Calvin died

Calvinist churches were established across Europe

in 1564, Calvinist churches had been established across Europe—they existed in the Netherlands, France, England, Germany, and Scotland. Theodore Beza, an exiled French nobleman, who had been Calvin's right-hand man for 20 years, took his place as the leader of the branch of Protestantism called Calvinism.

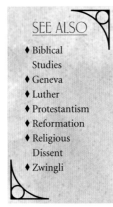

SEE ALSO
◆ Biblical Studies
◆ Geneva
◆ Luther
◆ Protestantism
◆ Reformation
◆ Religious Dissent
◆ Zwingli

Capitalism

Capitalism is the economic system under which most of the Western world operates today. It involves the use of capital—money and equipment—to produce goods that are then sold in markets. The capital involved is usually owned by one person or by a company and not by the people involved in producing the goods—the workers.

In the Middle Ages most goods had been produced on a small scale in villages or craft workshops for local people. The craftsman usually owned his own tools and was master of his own enterprise. He only produced enough goods to sell locally and made a modest living.

A system called mercantilism was a forerunner of capitalism. It can be roughly defined as the redistribution of goods for profit. Under the mercantile system, which medieval Europeans learned from the Islamic peoples during the Crusades, a merchant bought goods in one place and then moved them to another place, where he sold them at a higher price than he had paid for them—so making a profit. The term mercantilism later grew to have a different meaning, describing a form of economic policy in which governments tried to hold as much gold and silver as possible by increasing exports and decreasing imports. This policy was popular between the 16th and 18th centuries.

TAKING RISKS

Merchants could make a lot of money, but they also incurred heavy risks. They often had to borrow money to buy the goods, and there was a very real danger that ships carrying their goods from one country to another might be sunk, with the loss of the cargo, or that overland trade routes might be attacked by robbers.

To minimize these risks, merchants began to band together into companies.

Below: Merchants are shown hard at work in this illustration from a 15th-century manuscript. The one on the left is selling food; the one in the middle is dealing in grain; while the one on the right is a money-lender.

These companies had offices in a network of cities and so were well placed to oversee trade in the various regions where the company operated. A large company also generated large amounts of money, which meant it could make large loans to a ruler in return for valuable trading concessions.

EARLY CAPITALISM

The capitalist system had many similarities with mercantilism. Both setups were concerned with buying and selling goods for profit. But while the merchant simply bought ready-made goods and sold them on, the capitalist began to control the means of production.

This happened first in agriculture. Some manorial lands were bought up by rich merchants in the late 14th century and farmed to produce cash crops such as grain or wool. The peasants lost their rights to their own strips of land. Some were hired to work on their former manor for wages; others drifted to the cities, where they hoped to find work.

The organization of the cloth industry was another example of early capitalism. In the 15th century Italy was famous for its rich, patterned silks, sometimes woven with gold or silver threads. These silk fabrics were sold all over Europe. However, the production of such luxury items involved a considerable capital outlay. The raw silk had to be brought in from abroad, and the costs of the other materials used—expensive dyes, the alum used as a fixative for the colors, and gold and silver thread—also amounted to a great deal of money.

Right: A 15th-century illustration of the interior of a fabric shop showing a range of brightly colored silks. Dyeing and weaving silk demanded a huge capital outlay, and wealthy merchant-bankers gradually took control of silk production during the Renaissance.

THE RURAL PUTTING-OUT SYSTEM

In the Renaissance period most clothes were made of wool. The processing of raw wool into cloth involved a number of stages, which in an earlier time had all been carried out in one peasant household. However, it became the practice for a merchant to buy up a quantity of raw wool and to "put it out" to rural artisans who would carry out the following processes.

Preparing the wool: First, the wool had to be sorted and washed; then it was carded, which involved straightening out all the curled and knotted fibers.

Spinning: The wool was then delivered to country-women who would spin it into yarn, using a distaff or a spinning wheel.

Weaving: The yarn was delivered to weavers, who generally owned their own looms. The weavers wove the yarn into cloth and were usually paid on a piece-work basis.

Finishing: This involved several processes, such as fulling and tentering (stretching). The processes were carried out by skilled craftsmen, some in a small water-driven mill and others at home.

Dyeing: Wool could be dyed either as yarn or after it was woven. Dyers were specialized craftsmen who often worked for several cloth manufacturers.

Under the putting-out system the merchant bought the raw wool and owned the product throughout all its stages of production. Rural craftsmen and women

Above: An illustration from a 15th-century calendar showing a countrywoman working at home, using a distaff to spin raw wool into yarn. A different worker would weave the yarn into cloth.

worked on goods that did not belong to them, and eventually they became completely financially dependent on the merchant.

So it became the practice for a merchant-banker to control the operation. He had the financial resources to pay out the large amount of capital needed to buy all the necessary materials. He then supervised the production process, putting the raw silk out to skilled dyers and weavers, and finally selling the finished product at a profit. A similar system operated in the production of woolen cloth (see box), which involved many separate processes.

EARLY INDUSTRIALIZATION

These methods of capitalist production were early examples of industrialization—the process of producing goods by breaking the method of production down into separate steps and employing different workers to carry out each step. The workers were often paid on piecework, which means they were not given a regular wage but were paid for the amount of work they had done. The workers involved in the early textile industries were still craftsmen, however, and many of them owned their own tools. They also worked in their own homes or craft shops. It was not until the 18th century that the Industrial Revolution brought about the kind of industry we know today, in which people are paid wages for working in a factory owned, together with the tools and equipment, by a capitalist.

SEE ALSO
♦ Agriculture
♦ Bankers and Banking
♦ Guilds and Crafts
♦ Manufacturing
♦ Merchants
♦ Textiles
♦ Trade
♦ Wealth

Catholic Church

Until the 16th century the Catholic church was probably the single most important and powerful institution in Renaissance Europe. As well as being essential to the spiritual welfare of the people, it was also extremely wealthy and was Europe's principal landowner.

The pope, who was the bishop of Rome, was elected by the cardinals and enjoyed a position of particular authority as the head of Christendom. In the Renaissance religion played a much more important role in people's lives than it does today. People were baptized as infants, then confirmed in the faith as adolescents, and finally received the last rites before dying. Marriages were conducted by the

Below: This 15th-century triptych (three-part painting) for a church altar shows the inside of a church with a crucifixion scene. The crucifixion of Christ was central to the Christian religion and was often painted in the Renaissance.

church, and many of the people who remained unmarried became priests, monks, or nuns. At least once a year church members confessed their sins to a priest and then took holy communion at the Mass.

The late 14th century saw the church in crisis. Partly because of the growing power of the French king, the eight popes who had reigned from 1309 to 1377 had lived in Avignon, in southern France. Many churchpeople feared that the French influence on the papacy was too great, and this period became known as the "Babylonian Captivity" of the church. Generally, the popes of Avignon seemed to have little concern for spiritual matters, and the great Italian poet Petrarch called Avignon the "sewer of the world."

separation) divided the church, and two popes claimed the right to reign. Each pope excommunicated—expelled from the church—the other. Most of western Europe supported Clement VII, who moved to Avignon, while central Europe generally allied with Urban VI, who remained in Rome. In many areas confusion reigned, and some parishes even had two priests, one who was loyal to Rome and the other to Avignon.

To resolve the situation, professors at the University of Paris proposed that a general council of the church be called to make a final decision. Hundreds of churchmen, bishops, and cardinals met at Pisa in 1409, although neither of the two popes accepted an invitation to attend. The council denounced both popes as heretics and elected a new pope, who became Alexander V (pope 1409–1410). Neither of the other popes paid any attention to the decrees of the Council of Pisa, and both refused to step down. Europe now had three popes.

Gregory XI (pope 1370–1378) moved the papacy back to Rome in 1377, but died early the following year. Rioting broke out in the streets of Rome, with people demanding that the papacy remain in their city and that the cardinals choose an Italian to be the new pope. Apparently unmoved by these demands, the cardinals chose Urban VI (pope 1378–1389), whose hometown of Naples had ties to France, to be the next pope. However, within a month the cardinals sneaked out of Rome, announced that Urban's election was invalid because of the threats of the Roman mob, and chose another pope, who reigned as Clement VII (1378–1394).

Above: A 14th-century illustration of the coronation of Pope Clement VII in 1378.

THE GREAT SCHISM

The existence of two popes seriously undermined the papacy's claim to be the single religious authority in the Christian world. From 1378 to 1417 a debate known as the Great Schism (or

CONCILIARISM

Until the time of the Great Schism the pope had been the undisputed head of the Catholic church. But in order to end the situation of having more than one pope, church lawyers argued the case for conciliarism. The policy of conciliarism meant that a general council of the church could make decisions that could override those of the pope.

In 1409 the Council of Pisa attempted to depose both rival popes, but neither would accept its authority. However, when the Council of Constance met in 1414, it passed a number of resolutions to ensure that a crisis like the Great Schism could not occur again. It declared that in the future the council of the church should meet at regular intervals as a kind of governing body of the church, and that its authority should be greater than that of the pope. This doctrine of conciliarism greatly reduced the power of the papacy.

Right: Sigismund, king of Germany, is shown presiding over the Council of Constance in this illustration from a 15th-century manuscript. Sigismund called the council in 1414 to try to resolve the dispute over which of the three popes should reign.

Sigismund, king of Germany and future Holy Roman emperor (ruled 1410–1437), summoned a new council, which met in the German city of Constance in 1414. The Council of Constance declared its own authority to be greater than any pope's. Two of the existing popes were deposed, and the third abdicated. The council chose an Italian cardinal, Martin V (pope 1417–1431), to replace them, and the Great Schism was finally over.

CORRUPTION IN THE CHURCH

The Great Schism did considerable damage to the church at a time when it already had many opponents. Critics felt that the church was too highly involved in everyday politics and that too many of its priests used their position to build up their own wealth and power.

One person who held these views was the Czech reformer Jan Hus (about 1372–1415). He was strongly influenced by the English reformer John Wycliffe (about 1330–1384), who taught that the government could legally take over the salaries of immoral priests and that the pope had no authority outside of purely spiritual matters. Because of his teachings Hus had been excommunicated (banned from the church) in 1414. He hoped to put his case before the Council of Constance and was given a guarantee of safety by Sigismund. Despite this, Hus was arrested and tried for heresy in

1414. Refusing to take back his teachings, he was burned at the stake. This betrayal sparked a violent revolution by his supporters in Bohemia.

CHALLENGING THE POPE'S POWER

Many of the decrees of the Council of Constance reappeared in special treaties, called concordats, between the papacy and various national governments. Once supreme as the head of Christendom, the pope had become something like an equal to the kings of Europe. A new church council opened in what was then the German city of Basel in 1431. Eugene IV (pope 1431–1447), who was opposed to the council,

Below: A picture from a 15th-century book of hours (prayer book), which shows death as a skeletally thin man carrying the symbols of his trade—a sickle and huge arrows. Illustrations of death were very common in Renaissance times.

moved it to Ferrara in Italy. But those participants supporting conciliarism (see box on page 27) resented Eugene IV's interference and elected their own pope, Felix V (pope 1439–1449).

The election of Felix V did not cause a second great schism, however, because the various national governments refused to support a pope chosen by a council. The rulers of Europe had come to see conciliarism as a threat to their own authority; if a council could remove a pope, what could stop it from removing a king?

These issues with church leadership and unity were not the worst problems Christians had to face during the late 14th century, however. Famine, warfare, and economic depression were accompanied, after 1347, by the plague known as the Black Death.

DEATH AND THE AFTERLIFE

Except for the 20th century, no era saw more widespread premature death in Europe than the Renaissance, and perhaps no time saw a more intense fear of death and sin. Death was often depicted in religious art, and books giving advice on preparing for death were bestsellers.

The church provided several aids to help Christians cope with the hardships of their lives. Some Christians made pilgrimages to shrines to pray for help. Others collected relics—objects associated with the life of Christ or the saints, which were believed to have special powers. The Elector Frederick of Saxony, for example, made a pilgrimage to Jerusalem and owned a collection of relics that included straw supposedly from the stable where Christ was born. People could ask for help from saints for various sicknesses—from Saint Roche for the plague or Saint Blaise for a sore throat.

Left: The Council of Trent, recorded in a 16th-century painting. The council was a series of conferences held between 1545 and 1563 in Trent, Italy, to counteract Protestantism and clarify the teachings of the Catholic church.

One young student named Martin Luther (1483–1546) promised Saint Anne that he would become a monk if she saved his life in a violent thunderstorm. He kept his vow, and as a monk he worried constantly about how his sins would affect his life after death. After studying the Bible carefully, Luther came to believe that the gift of God's grace, received through faith, was more important for salvation than his own personal efforts.

Luther preached against the practice of selling indulgences (cancelations of punishment for sins) and eventually attacked the authority of the pope, who excommunicated him in 1521. Other reformers, such as John Calvin and Huldreich Zwingli, also attacked the church. Although there were important differences between the various Protestant reformers, they all emphasized the importance of the Bible as the basis of Christianity. They also generally agreed on the doctrine of salvation by faith alone (rather than good works) and spoke out against corruption within the church.

By the middle of the 16th century much of northern Europe had become Protestant and no longer recognized the authority of the Catholic pope. In an effort to win back some of these lost lands, the church initiated a movement to fight Protestantism. The church also attempted to correct its faults.

THE COUNTER REFORMATION

The Counter Reformation movement, as it became known, grew especially strong during the reign of Paul III (pope 1534–1549). Paul encouraged the growth of new religious orders, such as the Jesuits, and called the Council of Trent (1545–1563), which clarified the teachings of the Catholic church without yielding to the Protestant challenges.

Other measures of the Counter Reformation were more aggressive, including the founding of a new Inquisition and an Index of Forbidden Books (1542). A new spirituality developed, especially in Spain, which nurtured the saints Theresa of Avila and John of the Cross.

Cellini

Benvenuto Cellini (1500–1571) was one of the most colorful artists of the 16th century. He was the greatest Italian goldsmith of his time, an outstanding sculptor, and the author of a famous autobiography that gives a richly entertaining account of his life.

Although he was born in Florence, where he worked for the city's powerful ruling family the Medici, Cellini had many other important patrons. They included several popes in Rome and King Francis I of France, and Cellini rarely stayed in one place for more than a few years. His restlessness was partly caused by his violent and vain personality, which made him enemies wherever he went. He had several brushes with the law, and in 1534 he killed a rival goldsmith in Rome—although he was pardoned by his loyal patron Pope Paul III. These and other escapades are described in vivid detail in Cellini's autobiography, which often reads like a sensational novel.

GOLDSMITH AND SCULPTOR

Cellini was a versatile and highly skilled artist. He produced work in many different materials—including gold, bronze, and marble—and in many different sizes, ranging from medals to larger-than-life statues. All are highly sophisticated and elegant, created with meticulous attention to detail and a polished finish.

Cellini's work includes some of the most refined examples of mannerism, a style that was popular in Florence and

Left: Cellini's bronze sculpture **Perseus and Medusa,** *made between 1545 and 1554. The elegant pose and attention to detail are typical of Cellini's work.*

Rome in the middle of the 16th century. Mannerist artists exaggerated appearances to make the figures and objects they portrayed look more elegant.

In 1543 Cellini created the most famous piece of goldsmith's work to survive from the Renaissance—a gold saltcellar for King Francis I of France. It was designed to hold salt and pepper and to act as a lavish centerpiece at banquets. It is about 12 in. (30cm) in length and is adorned with two elegant, reclining figures who represent the earth and the sea. The figures' graceful poses and their smoothly finished and slightly elongated bodies are typical of the mannerist style.

PERSEUS AND MEDUSA

Cellini's most famous sculpture, *Perseus and Medusa*, was made between 1545 and 1554 for Cosimo de Medici, the ruler of Florence. In Greek mythology Perseus was a hero who killed Medusa, a snake-haired female monster known as a gorgon who could turn men to stone simply by looking at them. Cellini portrays Perseus in his moment of triumph, holding up the severed head of Medusa, his left foot resting on her body. The graceful pose of Perseus's muscular body is matched by the carefully finished details, such as his winged helmet and curling hair.

SEE ALSO

♦ Decorative Arts
♦ Guilds and Crafts
♦ Mannerism
♦ Sculptors' Materials and Techniques
♦ Sculpture

Cervantes

The Spanish writer Miguel de Cervantes Saavedra (1547–1616) wrote one of the most famous novels of all time. *Don Quixote* was not only very popular in its day; it also proved to be hugely influential on the development of the novel.

Cervantes's early life was very eventful. As a young man he took part in the great naval battle of Lepanto, fought in 1571 between the Spanish and the Ottoman Turks. Despite suffering from a fever, he displayed remarkable bravery during the fighting.

Cervantes stayed in the army until 1575. Then, when he was on his way back to Spain, his ship was captured by pirates, and he and his brother Rodrigo were sold into slavery in Algiers.

Left: Statues of Don Quixote (left) and his squire Sancho Pancha (right), the main characters in Cervantes' great novel. Quixote's adventures include mistaking windmills for giants and flocks of sheep for armies.

He was held for ransom, but it was five years before his family managed to raise the money.

When Cervantes returned to Spain in 1580, he became a civil servant, at first requisitioning supplies of corn and oil for the Spanish Armada, and later becoming a tax collector. All this time, however, he was writing, trying his hand at poetry, plays, and short stories. Cervantes eventually found success in 1605 with the publication of *The Ingenious Hidalgo Don Quixote of La Mancha, Part I*, better known simply as *Don Quixote*.

LITERARY SUCCESS

The novel tells about the adventures of an elderly man who is a lover of tales of chivalry and decides to live the life of a medieval knight. The foolish, deluded Don Quixote quickly became a popular figure, half-comic, half-tragic. By the end of the year several new editions of the book had appeared across Spain. It was soon published abroad as well. Because Cervantes had sold the copyright outright, however, he made no more money from the book.

Cervantes now began to write almost full time. He published a brilliant collection of short stories in 1613, a long satirical poem called *Journey to Parnassus* in 1614, and a collected edition of his plays in 1615. In the same year he also published the second part of *Don Quixote*. His last work was a heroic romance called *The Labors of Persiles and Sigismunda*. He wrote the dedication only three days before his death on April 22, 1616.

SEE ALSO

♦ Chivalry
♦ Literature

Charles V

The Holy Roman emperor Charles V (1500–1558) was the most powerful European ruler of his day. He was a member of the Hapsburg family, and his position was the result of the clever diplomatic strategy of his ancestors, who through marriage had created a network of alliances among some of the most important royal families in Europe. Although his lands had been acquired largely by peaceful means, Charles spent almost his entire reign at war as he tried to protect them.

Charles became king of Spain in 1516. He inherited this title from his grandparents on his mother's side, Ferdinand II and Isabella I. Charles's other grandfather was the Holy Roman emperor Maximilian I. Maximilian could not automatically pass on his title to his grandson, since the emperor had to be elected. However, one of Maximilian's wealthy supporters managed to secure the position for Charles, who took it in 1519. From Maximilian's wife, Mary of Burgundy, Charles inherited large areas of northwestern Europe, including the wealthy region of the Netherlands. Charles also ruled Austria and parts of Germany and Italy.

Although Charles' lands gave him an enormous amount of political and military power, he had a large number of enemies. The most important of these opponents was the French king Francis I (1515–1547). Charles' control

Below: A portrait of Charles V, who was elected Holy Roman emperor in 1519. Charles was a member of the powerful Hapsburg family, which had ruled the Holy Roman Empire since 1438.

THE REVOLT OF THE *COMUNEROS*

Charles V grew up in the Netherlands; and when he arrived in Spain in 1517 to be crowned king of Spain, he met with a great deal of opposition. The Spanish people regarded him as a foreigner, who spoke virtually no Spanish, and had no experience in government. To make matters worse, he installed many non-Spaniards in positions of power. When Charles tried to raise taxes to help cover the cost of his campaign to be elected Holy Roman emperor, the *comuñeros* (town governments) rose up in revolt.

Charles had returned to Germany after spending two and a half years in Spain when the revolt happened. Spain was being ruled by Adrian of Utrecht—Charles' former tutor who was later to be Pope Adrian VI—whom Charles had installed as regent. When the revolt began to threaten Spain's nobility as well, the nobles joined forces with Adrian to crush it brutally. The towns never again threatened the king.

In the following years Charles took steps to develop a closer bond with his Spanish subjects, promoting native Spaniards to important government positions. For much of the rest of his reign Charles' Spanish lands provided both the bulk of the soldiers and the finances for his extensive wars.

of Spain, Austria, and the Netherlands meant that France was encircled by lands belonging to Charles' family— the Hapsburgs. Because of this threat Francis had unsuccessfully attempted to convince the electors to choose him as emperor rather than Charles.

However, the rivalry between the French and Spanish kings did not end with Charles' election as emperor. The tension between the two rulers eventually resulted in open warfare when Charles attacked France in 1521. This assault marked the beginning of a long period of war.

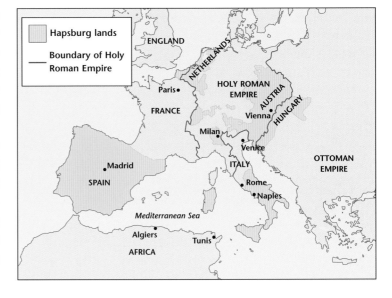

WAR WITH FRANCE

In 1524 Francis led his armies into Italy, where he attacked and took Milan, which was under Charles' control and had long been a point of contention between the two countries. In order to take the city back, Charles led an army from his German territories and defeated the French at the Battle of Pavia in 1525. Francis was taken prisoner and forced to sign a treaty, giving up his claims to Charles' lands.

Despite the treaty, the two countries were soon at war again. Within months

of his release in 1526 Francis had entered into an anti-Hapsburg alliance with Pope Clement VII, King Henry VIII of England, and several northern Italian cities. The alliance was known as the League of Cognac.

When Charles found out about the alliance, he led an army to attack Rome and captured it. A large part of the city was destroyed, and many people were killed. Pope Clement himself was forced to flee.

Charles and the pope finally made peace in 1529, when Clement officially

Above: A map showing the extent of the Hapsburg territories and the Holy Roman Empire during the reign of Charles V.

crowned Charles emperor in Bologna. It was to be the last time a Holy Roman emperor was crowned by a pope. Later that year Charles also made a temporary peace with Francis.

THE OTTOMANS

France, however, was not Charles' only enemy. To the southeast of Europe lay the mighty empire of the Ottoman Turks. Since the beginning of the 16th century the Ottoman Empire had been growing rapidly.

After the great sultan Suleyman the Magnificent (about 1494–1566) gained power in 1520, the Ottomans pushed farther into Europe. In the early years of Suleyman's reign they advanced into Hungary. By 1529 they had reached as far west as the Hapsburg city of Vienna, which they unsuccessfully besieged.

Three years later Charles was forced to march with a large army to defend Vienna from another Ottoman attack. After a stalemate the Ottoman forces eventually retreated.

However, Charles had to contend not only with attacks against his eastern lands. For most of his reign he was also engaged in a naval struggle with the Ottoman Turks for control of the Mediterranean Sea.

THE WAR AT SEA

Since the turn of the century the Ottomans had conquered much of the north coast of Africa, which gave them a considerable amount of control over Mediterranean trade.

In 1535 Charles attacked and captured the Ottomans' Mediterranean power base, the city of Tunis. He also

Below: This 16th-century painting portrays Charles V (right) talking to Pope Clement VII. Clement shifted sides repeatedly in the struggle between Charles and the French king Francis I.

Right: The war between the armies of the Ottoman sultan Suleyman the Magnificent and Charles V is depicted in this large wall painting from a villa in Florence.

attacked Algiers six years later. Despite these successes, Charles never seriously managed to threaten Ottoman influence in the Mediterranean.

THE THREAT OF PROTESTANTISM

Some of the most important struggles of Charles' reign, however, were carried out within the Holy Roman Empire itself. In 1517, two years before Charles was elected emperor, a German priest named Martin Luther (1483–1546) directly challenged the Catholic church, saying it was corrupt. His views quickly found a great deal of popular support. Almost from the very day that Charles was elected emperor, he found himself at the forefront of a battle between Catholicism and Protestantism, the branch of Christianity that developed from Luther's beliefs.

In 1521 Martin Luther was forced to appear at the Diet (assembly) in the city of Worms to explain his teachings to Charles as Holy Roman emperor. Luther refused to apologize for his beliefs, and Charles and the assembly issued the Edict of Worms. The edict condemned Luther's views, forbade his writings, and made him an outlaw.

The Edict of Worms drew a clear battle line between Charles and Catholicism on one side and Luther and Protestantism on the other. However,

---

Charles found himself at the forefront of the battle between Catholicism and Protestantism

---

the political situation in Europe made the issue more complicated. As Holy Roman emperor, Charles supposedly ruled Germany. Most of the German princes whose lands were part of the empire were powerful enough to be practically independent, however, and many of them were supporters of Luther. Since Charles needed the aid of these princes in his struggles against

France and the Ottomans, he had to be careful not to alienate them too much.

In 1530 the Catholic church issued another proclamation, known as the Confutation, which echoed the 1521 Edict of Worms. In response a number of Protestant German cities and principalities joined together to form the Schmalkaldic League. The league posed a serious threat to Charles, but he was preoccupied with the Ottomans and could not afford to fight two enemies at once.

Charles did not finally confront the Schmalkaldic League until 1547. Three years earlier another prolonged period of war with France had ended with the Truce of Crespy, and Charles could finally concentrate on his Protestant enemies in the north. He led a Spanish army over the Alps and defeated the Protestants at the Battle of Mühlberg.

After Mühlberg Charles took some steps toward healing the rift between the Protestants and the Catholics and reuniting the empire, but they were unsuccessful. In 1551 Henry II, the son of Francis I and the new king of France, made an alliance with the northern German princes, leading to yet another war. Faced by the strength of this rebel alliance, Charles was forced to sign an agreement that gave Protestants equal rights to Catholics.

THE FINAL YEARS

Suffering with gout and exhausted by marching and countermarching with his troops across the face of Europe for so many years, Charles decided to abdicate in 1555. He divided his lands between his son Philip, who inherited the Netherlands and Spain, and his brother Ferdinand, who took control of the Hapsburg lands in Germany and central Europe. Charles then retired to the monastery at Yuste, in the mountains to the west of Madrid, where he spent his final years. He died in 1558.

Left: A 16th-century wall painting showing Charles V (on the right in the black hat) riding into Paris, the capital of France, in 1540 beside his lifelong opponent King Francis I of France (on the left). War between the two men broke out again in 1542, but was finally ended by the Truce of Crespy in 1544.

Chaucer

Geoffrey Chaucer (about 1342–1400) was one of the most important writers in the history of English literature and the first great writer to write in the English language rather than Latin or French. His most famous work, *The Canterbury Tales*, is still widely read today.

Chaucer's father was a wealthy London wine merchant, and the family owned property in Ipswich and London. As a young man Chaucer served in the household of Elizabeth, countess of Ulster. He also fought in the Hundred Years' War between England and France, and served as a messenger to the king, Edward III. It was the first of many prestigious appointments held by Chaucer during his life. At various times he worked as a diplomat, customs officer, civil servant, justice of the peace, and member of parliament.

CHAUCER THE WRITER

It was during Chaucer's time in the household of Elizabeth of Ulster that he met the man who was later to become his chief patron—the nobleman John of Gaunt, duke of Lancaster. Chaucer's first major work, the *Book of the Duchess*, was written after John's wife had died of the plague. The poem was written in the style of a "dream vision" in which the narrator falls asleep, and his dreams form the story. It was published in either 1369 or 1370.

Unlike most of his contemporaries, who wrote either in Latin or French, Chaucer chose to write in English. He showed that the English language was subtle, flexible, and expressive enough to be used for sophisticated literature. In the *Book of the Duchess* Chaucer catches the vigor and rhythm of natural English speech within the strict structure of the verse.

As a result of the various positions that he held, Chaucer traveled widely throughout Europe. In particular, he spent a considerable amount of time in Italy. There he came into contact with the work of writers such as Petrarch and Boccaccio, who had a considerable influence on him. Chaucer's next great work was *Troilus and Criseyde*, a version of one of the stories in Boccaccio's *Decameron*. Set during the Trojan War, *Troilus and Criseyde* is the tragic account of a young man betrayed by his lover, told in poetic form.

Although to some scholars *Troilus and Criseyde* is Chaucer's greatest work,

Above: A portrait of Geoffrey Chaucer, one of the greatest writers in the history of the English language. Chaucer held many public offices, which enabled him to travel widely and meet people from all levels of European society.

most give that honor to *The Canterbury Tales*, built around a group of pilgrims traveling from London to Canterbury. On the journey the pilgrims take turns entertaining one another with stories.

Chaucer did not have time to complete *The Canterbury Tales* before his death in 1400. Nevertheless, it remains one of the most important works in the history of English literature.

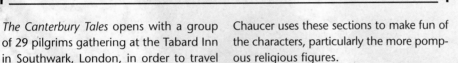

THE CANTERBURY TALES

The Canterbury Tales opens with a group of 29 pilgrims gathering at the Tabard Inn in Southwark, London, in order to travel to Canterbury to visit the shrine of the murdered archbishop Thomas à Beckett. The pilgrims represent a cross-section of society—among them are a knight, a miller, a prioress, a merchant, and a monk.

To amuse themselves on the way, the pilgrims agree to tell one another stories. They are as varied as the pilgrims' personalities, allowing Chaucer to explore different literary styles. Some tales are coarse and comic, while others deliver a serious religious message. Lively exchanges between the various pilgrims link the tales.

Chaucer uses these sections to make fun of the characters, particularly the more pompous religious figures.

Originally, *The Canterbury Tales* was supposed to cover the pilgrims' journey to Canterbury and their return to London, with each pilgrim telling two tales. However, the work remained unfinished at the time of Chaucer's death, and only 24 tales were written, four of which remain incomplete.

Below: A 15th-century illustration of pilgrims on the road to Canterbury. Chaucer's pilgrims were a mixed group, from all levels of society.

SEE ALSO
- Boccaccio
- Literature
- Petrarch
- Poetry

Children

Children and young people made up a large proportion of the population in Renaissance Europe; in some countries nearly half the inhabitants were aged under 25. At the same time, the rates of infant mortality (death) were extremely high —up to half the children died before reaching adulthood.

In Renaissance times parents exercised absolute authority, making important decisions about their children's lives— from education to choice of profession and marriage partner. Discipline was harsh, and it was considered acceptable to beat children. Childhood was short by today's standards, and many children had to work by the time they were seven years old.

CHILDREN OF THE POOR

The vast majority of the population (about 90 percent) still lived on the land. For children of the very poorest laborers and tenant farmers life was a struggle. From as young as seven they helped their parents in a variety of ways—they were stationed in fields of newly sown grain to scare away the

Above: This painting by the 16th-century Flemish artist Pieter Bruegel the Elder shows a crowd of childen at play. They are enjoying all kinds of games—including ones like leapfrog that are still played today.

birds; they were put in charge of grazing cattle and sheep; they fed ducks and chickens and collected their eggs; and they milked cows and goats. Girls were expected to help their mothers with household tasks such as cleaning, washing clothes, cooking, spinning yarn,

---

Poor children had few clothes or toys and slept on straw mattresses

---

and sewing clothes for all the family. The children of the poorest laborers were sent away from home to work for richer yeoman farmers.

Poor children had few clothes or toys and slept on straw mattresses in crowded haylofts or storerooms. The very poorest children could expect little or no education. If they were lucky, a parish priest might teach them the rudiments of reading and writing, but many remained illiterate.

In towns the sons of laborers and craftsmen were frequently signed up as apprentices. For a period of seven years they were taught every aspect of a trade such as cobbling or leatherworking. Apprenticeships were hard, but they led to certain employment. Once the boys were earning money, they could begin to save for their future—young men frequently did not marry until they were in their late twenties.

Girls in towns were not so fortunate. Like their country counterparts, they stayed at home and were kept busy with household tasks until, at the age of 16 or 17, they were ready for marriage.

High rates of illness and death (especially in childbirth) meant that many poor children were orphaned at an early

age. If they were lucky, they were taken into care by a guardian appointed by the village community.

In towns orphaned children or those abandoned by parents who could no longer cope were placed in the local poorhouse, orphanage, or foundling hospital. There the children received a basic education, and many foundling boys went on to become apprentices. Orphaned or abandoned children who had no one to care for them became child beggars, wandering from village to village, scavenging for food such as fallen fruit and acorns.

WEALTHY FAMILIES

Life was much easier for the children of the increasingly wealthy section of society—including yeomen (landowning farmers), merchants, and professionals such as doctors and lawyers. Babies from

Above: This wall painting from the 15th century shows orphaned children being cared for in a foundling hospital. Older children received some basic education, and many of the boys were apprenticed to learn a craft.

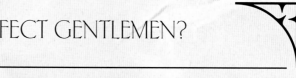

PERFECT GENTLEMEN?

It is hardly surprising that young noblemen sometimes broke away from the constraints of their education by forming gangs and loyal brotherhoods that were frequently involved in rivalries, violence, and disturbances. They were vividly depicted by Shakespeare in the conflict between the Montagues and Capulets in his play *Romeo and Juliet*. In one notorious incident in Florence in 1420 a gang of youths seized the body of an executed man who had been a prominent member of a rival clan. They cut off the hands, used them as footballs, and prevented the corpse from being buried for four days.

Below: In this illustration from a 15th-century French manuscript noble girls are shown learning to spin and weave, while their brothers practice swordplay and wrestling.

well-to-do families were sent to wet nurses, who breast-fed and looked after them until they were at least 18 months old. When they returned home to their families, they enjoyed an all too brief childhood. They played with toys, such as rocking horses, tambourines, drums, wooden soldiers, stilts, balls, and shuttlecocks, and were allowed to keep pets like dogs, cats, and caged birds.

Children from wealthy families began their education young and were often taught the rudiments of reading and writing, and Latin and Greek, by a hired tutor at home. By the time they were eight, many sons had been sent away to school, where they were taught Latin, Greek, history, geography, arithmetic, astronomy, music, and languages. This well-rounded education prepared them for college and entry into the professions. Girls were more likely to see their education cut short; they were kept at home until they were old enough to be married.

THE NOBILITY

The medieval practice of sending sons from noble families away to serve as pages in other noble households was replaced in the Renaissance by a renewed emphasis on education. Sons of the aristocracy were prepared for the life of a courtier, and education was recognized as a means of advancement.

However, an academic education was only one part of the preparation for court life. Aristocrats were expected to be well-versed in poetry, dancing, and music, as well as being fit, sporting, and competitive. In the words of Roger Ascham, tutor to Queen Elizabeth I of England, a young man should be taught "to ride comely, to run fair at the tilt or ring, to play at all weapons . . . to wrestle, to swim, to dance comely, to sing and play of instruments cunningly, to hawk, to hunt, to play tennis."

China

Left: The Forbidden City in Beijing, where China's emperors lived. The city was built during the Ming emperor Ch'eng-tsu's reign (1403–1425) and was called the Forbidden City because only the emperor and his household were allowed to enter— everyone else was forbidden.

During the time of the Renaissance in Europe China was ruled by the Ming dynasty (1368–1644). Following more than 100 years of Mongol occupation of China, the 16 Ming emperors presided over one of the country's most stable and long-lasting dynasties. Improvements in agriculture supported a doubling of the population, and commerce and culture flourished. During the time of the Ming dynasty many surrounding regions paid tribute to China, which became a powerful and dominant influence in East Asia.

In the early 14th century Mongol control of China was crumbling. A peasant from southern China named Chu Yuan-chang (1328–1398) joined the Red Turbans, a revolutionary movement, and soon became one of their military

ABSOLUTE POWER

In Ming China the state had complete control over people's lives, and Chu Yuan-chang had complete control of the state. Learning from the collapse of Mongol rule in China, Chu outlawed radical groups, such as the one that had brought him to power. He supported Confucianism as the country's official religion, but only after he had deleted those parts of Confucian literature that condemned an absolute ruler. He set up an extensive spy network to watch his officials, and anyone who seemed to be acting suspiciously could be publicly beaten to death. In a reign of terror he had up to 100,000 political and military figures executed.

In 1380 Chu abolished the imperial secretariat (the country's main administrative body) and took a hands-on approach to government. This course of action involved an enormous amount of work—Chu once managed to work through documents dealing with 3,391 separate issues in just 10 days. Although he eventually appointed four grand secretaries to assist him, Chu insisted on ruling without a chancellor, whom he feared might challenge his authority.

commanders. He captured Nanking, made it his base, and set up a form of government based on the traditional imperial government. By 1368 Chu had driven the Mongol emperor out of China and established a new dynasty, the Ming, centered at Nanking.

LAYING THE FOUNDATIONS

During his 30-year reign (1368–1398) Chu was a tough ruler, bringing stability and prosperity to China. But he was a hard, cruel man, who insisted on absolute power (see box on page 43).

Strengthening the army and securing China's borders were Chu's first priorities. He then turned his attention to internal affairs. He restored the examination system for appointing the 20,000 officials who ran the civil service. In the countryside he organized

Above: A map showing the extent of the Ming Empire at the height of its power.

Left: The beautiful blue-and-white decoration of this elegant vase makes it typical of Ming period porcelain.

every 100 families into a unit called a "*li*"—if anyone behaved badly, the entire *li* was held responsible. Members of the *li* had to take turns filling local government offices, for which they were not paid.

BUILDING ON SUCCESS

Chu's successor as emperor, Ch'eng-tsu (ruled 1403–1425), was another good administrator. Ch'eng-tsu was responsible for launching military campaigns against the Mongols to the north and to subdue Vietnam in the south. He was also eager to promote trade and ordered a series of naval expeditions along known trade routes to establish good diplomatic relations with distant countries (see box).

In 1421 Ch'eng-tsu moved the capital to Peking (present-day Beijing) and rebuilt the Grand Canal to improve the transportation system. Although just as ruthless as Chu, Ch'eng-tsu also sponsored important scholarly publications, including a vast encyclopedia that kept 3,000 scholars occupied for five years.

After the death of Ch'eng-tsu China enjoyed a period of relative peace and prosperity. Departing from the practice

---

Some of the finest blue-and-white Ming ceramics date from Emperor Hsuan-tsung's reign

---

of his predecessors, the new emperor, Hsuan-tsung (ruled 1426–1435), allowed the influence of the court officials to grow. He also allowed the ministers of the grand secretariat to take over many of the duties of government. A talented poet and painter, Hsuan-tsung supported other artists at his court, and some of the finest blue-and-white Ming ceramics date from his reign.

The Mongols, however, continued to harass China. While inspecting border defenses, the emperor Ying-tsung (ruled 1436–1449 and 1457–1464)

Above: Chinese peasants gathering the rice harvest. Rice was the main food crop grown in Ming China.

was captured by the Mongols and held prisoner for over six years. After this embarrassing episode Ying-tsung and his successors rebuilt, fortified, and expanded the Great Wall along China's northern border.

DECAY AND REFORM

The emperors of the 16th century lacked the dedication of earlier Ming rulers, and the government earned a reputation for corruption and inefficiency. Emperors Wu-tsung (ruled 1506–1522) and Mu-tsung (ruled 1567–1572) were more concerned with having a good time than with governing; Shih-tsung (ruled 1522–1567) became obsessed with elaborate Taoist ceremonies, some of which could last several days. As the emperors' interest in government declined, the administration fell to the body of Confucian officials.

During this time several reformers appeared and proposed solutions for China's problems. The most famous

NAVAL EXPEDITIONS

From 1405 to 1433 the Chinese admiral Cheng Ho commanded seven naval expeditions to the Indian Ocean. The first voyage included almost 27,800 men serving on over 300 vessels—the greatest naval expedition the world had ever seen. The expeditions sailed to ports in Southeast Asia, India, the Persian Gulf, and East Africa. They established contact with foreign courts, more than 30 of which then sent envoys with presents back to China in order to do honor to the Ming court and to obtain trading rights. Giraffes from Africa became favorites of the emperor. Eventually, however, Mongol pressure in the north distracted the court from further naval expeditions, and China turned increasingly inward. All but four of Cheng's nautical charts were destroyed.

Above: This detail from a Ming vase shows women spinning silk, while a boy sits at their feet playing a flute.

nearly to his execution. Another reformer was Chang Chu-cheng (1525–1582), who held effective control of the government for many years.

Stressing the need for efficiency and strong government, Chang managed to keep the dynasty on a sound financial footing even while increasing military spending to deal with new threats from the Mongols. His other achievements included repairing the Great Canal and establishing silver as the basic unit of currency.

END OF THE MING

Despite the efforts of officials such as Chang, the Ming dynasty's grip on power weakened considerably toward the end of the 16th century. The imperial court increasingly became divided into rival factions. Corruption and high levels of taxation caused resentment among the poor and there were several large-scale rebellions. These revolts left the country destabilized and extremely vulnerable.

In 1644 a Ming general asked the Manchu people who lived on the southern steppes to help him put down

was Hai Jui (1513–1587), a magistrate who attempted to stamp out corruption and made tax duties more reasonable. With courage—or foolishness—he also denounced the emperor; Hai Jui's honesty led to imprisonment and

CHINESE RELIGIONS

The three main religious traditions of China—Taoism, Confucianism, and Buddhism—all prospered during the Ming dynasty. The Ming emperors appointed priests to administer Taoist rituals, which traced their origin to the philosopher Lao Tzu, who lived in the sixth century B.C. Lao Tzu had encouraged people to live simply, in accordance with the "Tao," or "Way," of nature.

Confucian philosophy was based on the teachings of Confucius, the most influential philosopher in Chinese history, who also lived during the sixth century B.C. Confucius had believed that both subjects and rulers should behave well and be brave, truthful, and polite to each other. Ming government officials

tried to follow the Confucian philosophy—but many of them also prayed to the god of scholars, Wen Ch'ang, before taking examinations.

Buddhism, which arose from the teachings of the Indian mystic the Buddha around 500 B.C., was also an important religion in China. The Buddha believed that misery was caused by attachment to the things of this world, and that if people could succeed in freeing themselves from wants and desires, they could find peace, or "enlightenment."

Other popular religious practices of the Ming period included the veneration of ancestors and household gods, as well as belief in ghosts and divination.

a rebellion. Instead, they took control of the country, establishing a new dynasty of their own—the Ch'ing.

AGRICULTURE AND TRADE

Farming was the main source of wealth in China, but under the Mongol occupation many areas had been devastated. The Ming rulers made great efforts to improve farming. Reservoirs and canals were built to help reclaim farmland, and people were moved into regions that had been depopulated. The government sponsored plans to build roads, plant trees to prevent soil erosion, keep granaries stocked in case of famine, and build dikes along the banks of the great rivers to prevent flooding. In addition, new varieties of rice were introduced that produced better yields. The result of all these measures was a great increase in agricultural output to the benefit of the whole population.

The state also encouraged the production of commercial crops for trade. They included silk—the silkworms grew on mulberry trees—and cotton. Silk was worn by wealthy Chinese and was also an important export.

Most of China's trade was internal; but following Cheng Ho's expeditions, trade with Southeast Asia increased. Porcelain, lacquer ware, tea, cotton, and silk were the main exports, which the Chinese traded for silver and spices.

FLOWERING OF THE ARTS

Under the Ming dynasty there was an increase in literacy, and Chinese literature flourished. Anthologies of short stories were favorites, and four important Ming novels are still popular today: *The Water Margin*, *The Romance of the Three Kingdoms*, *The Golden Lotus*, and *Journey to the West*. The last of them is a witty account of the

Buddhist monk Hsuan-tsang's journey to India, accompanied by a supernatural companion called Monkey, who protects the pilgrim monk from demons along the way. About 1,200 plays have also survived. Many are operatic dramas so long that usually only parts of them were performed.

Painting and calligraphy also flourished. Painters of the period, such as Lu Chi and Wen Cheng-ming, continued the Chinese tradition of painting with delicate brushstrokes to produce restful, decorative pictures of nature.

Above: A delicate painting of flowers and a pheasant by Lu Chi, from the Ming period.

SEE ALSO
♦ India
♦ Japan
♦ Trade

Left: This painting records the arrival in 1520 of King Henry VIII of England (bottom left) at a famous meeting with King Francis I of France. It was the occasion for nearly two weeks of chivalrous celebrations, including tournaments and jousting, and became known as the Field of the Cloth of Gold.

Chivalry

The concept of chivalry—the code of behavior knights were expected to follow—was extremely important in the Middle Ages. Among the qualities that knights were supposed to show were loyalty, courage, and compassion. Although knights no longer dominated the field of battle by the time of the Renaissance, the concept of chivalry remained popular.

Knights fought on horseback, and as heavily armored cavalry they were the most formidable part of any European army for several hundred years, from around the 10th century to the middle of the 14th century. They were better armed and more skilled than the soldiers who fought on foot. However, not just anyone could become a knight. Warhorses were extremely expensive to buy, as was armor. For this reason knights came almost exclusively from the ranks of the aristocracy.

CHIVALRY AND EDUCATION

In order to learn the skills necessary to fight as a knight, boys began training at the age of seven. It was during this time that they learned about the values of chivalry. Knights were supposed to protect the weak, show absolute loyalty to their lord or king, and be model Christians. In reality they often fell far short of these ideals, but the noble, courageous, generous knight became a popular figure in the stories and ballads of the time.

By the 15th century the knight was a far less important figure on the battlefield. Infantry, such as Swiss pikemen or English longbowmen, defeated armies based on mounted knights. When the use of guns and cannons began to become widespread in the second half of the 15th century, the knight's days were truly numbered. However skilled he was and however heavily armored, the knight could still be killed by a humble footsoldier armed with a gun.

TOURNAMENTS AND SOCIETIES

Even though the knight was no longer a force on the battlefield, the aristocracy still clung to the idea of chivalry. For example, tournaments continued to be very popular. The practice of knights fighting against each other in tournaments had begun in the 11th century, when the events were brutal mock battles with few rules. By the 15th century they had become extravagant spectacles in which noblemen could still fight each other, although under strict rules that lessened the likelihood of injury. These Renaissance tournaments allowed noblemen to display their wealth and to act out the life of a chivalrous knight without the risks involved in an actual war.

Another way in which the idea of chivalry lived on was in the orders of knights that became highly popular in the 15th century. These orders were exclusive societies of noblemen who

Chivalry lived on in the orders of knights that became popular in the 15th century

usually met once a year to feast and conduct religious ceremonies. The societies were based on the great fellowships of knights that had supposedly existed in the past, such as King Arthur's Knights of the Round Table.

As well as keeping chivalric values alive, the orders provided a way in which nobles could cement political alliances. Among the most important were the Order of the Garter, founded by Edward III of England in 1348, and the Order of the Golden Fleece, founded by Philip the Good of Burgundy in 1431.

SEE ALSO
♦ Arms and Armor
♦ Warfare

THE FAERIE QUEEN

Despite the decline of the knight as an effective soldier on the battlefield, tales of chivalry proved to be just as popular in the Renaissance as they had been in the medieval period. One of the most famous examples of this form of literature was the epic poem *The Faerie Queen*, written toward the end of the Renaissance period by the English poet Edmund Spenser (about 1552–1599). Incomplete at the time of Spenser's death, the poem was intended to be divided into 12 parts, each one recounting the adventures of a different knight, each knight representing a different virtue or quality. The success of Spenser's poem showed that the idea of chivalry was as popular at the end of the 16th century as it had been 500 years earlier.

Right: The title page of the first edition of **The Faerie Queene,** *published in 1590. Spenser's poem glorified Queen Elizabeth and extolled the virtues of chivalry.*

THE FAERIE
QVEENE.

Difpofed into twelue books,
Fafhioning
XII. Morall vertues.

LONDON
Printed for William Ponfonbie.

Christine de Pisan

Christine de Pisan (1364–1430) was an early European intellectual, a feminist, and the first European woman to make a living as a writer. In her lifetime she was famous across Europe for her poetry, essays, and fictional works. She was also one of the first female intellectuals to write about the issue of a woman's place in society.

Born in Venice, Christine grew up in Paris, where her father was court astrologer to the French king Charles V. Christine received an exceptional education for a woman of nonnoble birth, studying literature, mythology, history, and the sciences. In 1380 she married the court secretary Etienne du Castel. It was a happy marriage; but when Etienne died in 1390, Christine found herself a widow with no source of livelihood. To make matters worse, her mother and three children were dependent on her.

To support her family, Christine developed close ties with the royal family and other court nobles, hoping to benefit from her unusual status as an educated woman. She composed a number of poems in highly structured, complex verse, many dealing with her love for her husband and her grief at his death.

Like male poets of her time, Christine presented these early works as gifts to various court nobles, hoping for rewards in the form of cash or valuable objects such as jewels that she could sell. The emotional appeal and technical skill of her poems brought

Left: In this illustration from a 15th-century manuscript, Christine de Pisan kneels to present her work to King Charles VI of France. Christine's literary work was funded by commissions from Charles and other wealthy patrons.

her considerable fame, and soon she was able to support her family entirely through her commissions. Among her patrons were King Charles VI and Queen Isabeau of France, as well as the dukes of Burgundy and Berry.

WOMAN OF LETTERS

After 1400 Christine turned from poetry to prose, writing on a wide variety of topics, including her personal sufferings, politics, morals, religion, history, and the oppression of women. In 1404 she was commissioned by Duke Philip of Burgundy to write the official biography of Charles V.

In 1402 Christine gained more fame by participating with several male writers in a literary debate now called "The Quarrel of the Rose." In this debate she published letters challenging the negative attitudes toward women found in the popular poem *The Romance of the Rose*. It was one of the earliest Renaissance debates on the subject of women's equality.

Later, Christine composed an autobiography, and in a continued protest at the attitude of male writers she also produced her famous *Book of the City of Ladies* in 1405. A sequel, *The Book of the Three Virtues*, followed in 1406. *The City of Ladies* celebrates women's contributions to history and culture. In the book Christine makes an impassioned plea for women's education so that they can be better Christian wives and mothers. That would become a key argument in defense of women's rights in later Renaissance debates.

Christine was distraught over the destruction caused in France by the Hundred Years' War with England. Between 1410 and 1418 she composed *The Book of Peace, The Book of Feats of Arms and Chivalry*, and *Lamentations on the Civil War* to try to persuade France's leaders to rule peacefully.

In 1418 Christine retired to the convent of Poissy, where her daughter was a nun. She published only one work after

---

Admirers compared Christine to Cicero and Cato

---

that, *Hymn to Joan of Arc* (1429), about the military heroine who was bringing the hope of peace to the French people.

Christine de Pisan died sometime after 1430. Although her works were largely forgotten until the 20th century, contemporaries compared them to those of the Roman authors Cicero and Cato, and admirers had them translated and circulated outside France.

Left: An illustration showing Christine at her writing desk, guided and inspired by three women representing the virtues of prudence, justice, and honesty.

SEE ALSO

♦ Literature
♦ Patronage
♦ Poetry
♦ Women

City-States

During the Middle Ages the cities of northern and central Italy flourished. Many enjoyed political independence, each one forming the heart of a small city-state. These cities were ruled by councils rather than individual dukes and princes. During the Renaissance the larger and more powerful cities began to conquer their neighbors, while ambitious rulers and their families started to dominate the governments. However, smaller city-states continued to thrive.

From the 10th century the cities of northern and central Italy grew and prospered. Urban, or city-dwelling, populations swelled, and trade and manufacture boomed. Ports such as Venice, Genoa, and Pisa grew extremely rich importing and exporting spices and other goods. Some inland cities such as Siena, Vicenza, and Verona developed prosperous industries, notably woolen manufacture.

In central Italy Florence became an important banking as well as industrial center, while in the north Milan was a bustling river port. The cities of the south, such as Rome and Naples, fared less well. This was mainly because the region's poor farmlands were unable to provide either enough food to feed a large urban population or enough raw materials for industry.

Below: The Piazza del Mercato in the city of Lucca. Despite its small size, Lucca managed to retain its independence throughout the Renaissance.

By the mid-12th century most of the northern and central Italian cities had used their wealth to assert their political freedom from outside rule. For a long while both the German emperors of the Holy Roman Empire and the popes in Rome had competed for control over the cities. Now both

> *By the mid-12th century most of the northern and central Italian cities were free from outside rule*

these powers were in decline, and they were forced to allow the cities to be independent. These prosperous, free cities formed communes, or city-states. The communes controlled both the city itself and the surrounding countryside, called the *contado*. The *contado* provided the urban population with food, giving the cities a degree of self-sufficiency.

SYSTEMS OF GOVERNMENT

At first the communes were ruled by councils formed from three main groups: the land-owning noblemen from the *contado*; the local clergy; and the leading merchants, craftsmen, and bankers of the cities, who were also the heads of the local trade associations or merchant guilds. The prosperity and peace of the city depended on these groups working together, but they often came into conflict. In many places the guilds came to dominate the council and excluded members of the nobility and clergy from holding power. The ordinary inhabitants of the cities—who could include everyone from laborers to lawyers—usually had no political power.

During the 14th century the communes developed new forms of government. Strife between various factions in the cities meant that it was increasingly difficult for the civic authorities to keep peace. Their task was made harder by events taking place throughout Italy and in Europe at large. War, famine, and the Black Death all disrupted the prosperity of the Italian city-states.

In such circumstances many communes turned to an especially powerful and able individual to take control of the city. At first this was usually undertaken only as a temporary measure. However, once in power, a leader—or *signore*—was often

Above: This tablet from the biccherna, or revenue office, in Siena was painted in 1449. It shows the collection of taxes in peacetime and wartime.

THE CITY AND ART

Much of the culture of what we today call the Renaissance had its roots in the prosperous, competitive city-states of northern and central Italy. The city, the guilds, and the leading families used their excess wealth to buy goods—including tapestries, paintings, and sculptures—to enhance their standing. Cities competed not only to build the finest buildings but also to attract the best artists to decorate them. The splendor and cost of a painting or sculpture was a sign of civic pride. The civic authorities also funded schools and universities, and so helped create an educated, cultured ruling class who valued and enjoyed artistic achievements.

Below: A map of the Italian city-states in the late 15th century. By this time the larger city-states such as Venice and Milan had absorbed most of their smaller neighbors.

unwilling to give up his position. The *signori* usually overthrew or banished their opponents and handed down power to members of their own family. This new form of government was called a *signoria*.

One of the first *signorie* was formed in Milan, where Matteo Visconti (1250–1322) took power in 1311. Other *signorie* were established in Mantua, Verona, Cremona, Parma, and Vicenza, as well as in many other cities, especially in northern Italy. Despite their great power, the *signori* were not quite dictators. The old civic institutions—the council and its officers—usually continued to exist, though with fewer powers.

VENICE AND FLORENCE

Some of the most powerful city-states resisted the rise of signorial government and continued to be run as communes. Although Florence was ridden by strife, the sheer wealth and power of its leading merchants and bankers meant that it was hard for any one family to dominate the others. It was only with the arrival of the Medici in the mid-15th century that an individual family managed to take control of the city. Venice, on the other hand, was exceptionally peaceful and stable. Its inhabitants remained loyal to its civic leaders, including the city's largely symbolic head of state, the doge.

The inhabitants of the city-states had strong local ties and were very proud of their city's traditions. Their

Above: This early 16th-century painting shows Leonardo Loredan, who was doge of Venice between 1520 and 1521. The doge was the highest elected official in the republic of Venice.

sometimes decorated with frescoes that depicted important events in the city's history or expressed its ideals.

The cathedral was supposed to be under the control of the church, but the town council and the guilds had a great deal of say in how it was built and decorated because it was they who paid for the work. In 1418, for example, Florence's largest guild, the Wool Merchants, announced a competition for the construction of a dome for the city cathedral, Santa Maria dei Fiore. The spectacular dome that resulted— designed by Filippo Brunelleschi (1377–1446)—quickly became a symbol of the Florentines' civic pride.

Cities also managed to create a spirit of community through spectacular festivals and pageants or awe-inspiring religious processions. In Venice one such annual event was the Marriage with the Sea, during which the doge cast a gold ring into the lagoon as a symbol of the city's close relationship with the sea. In Siena colorful, exciting horse races were held on the main city square, the Piazza del Campo. Most of a city's inhabitants would come to watch such communal events, and amid the festivities differences were temporarily laid aside.

TERRITORIAL STATES

The spirit of rivalry between the Italian city-states also led to war, as neighboring cities competed with each other for land and resources. During the 14th and 15th centuries the most powerful city-states—Milan, Venice, and Florence—gradually extended their territories far beyond their *contadi* and conquered surrounding smaller, weaker city-states. For much of this period the three cities, together with the two other great powers in Italy, the Papal States and the kingdom of

fierce local patriotism expressed itself in the grandeur of a city's two most important buildings—the town hall (*palazzo comunale* or *palazzo publico*) and the cathedral. Cities competed with each other to build the biggest, the tallest, or the most lavish example of these buildings. This spirit of competition between Italian cities is sometimes known as *campanilismo*, from the Italian word *campanile*, meaning "bell-tower."

The town hall was the seat of the civic government. The town hall's public rooms often had copies of the city's statute books on display for any citizen to consult. Walls were

Naples in the south, were in almost constant conflict with one another. The allegiances between the five powers shifted continually.

THE RISE OF MILAN

The most aggressive city-state in the period of the Renaissance was Milan. In the late 14th century the *signore* of Milan, Gian Galeazzo Visconti (1351–1402), began to expand the area under the city's control. Visconti's family had ruled Milan since the late 13th century, when it had triumphed in a conflict between supporters of the pope,

---

> *Milan's armies seized many of the cities of northern Italy, creating a very powerful state*

---

known as Guelfs, and supporters of the Holy Roman emperor, such as the Visconti, known as Ghibelines. Gian Galeazzo Visconti was both ruthless and highly ambitious. From 1385 onward his armies seized many of the cities of northern Italy, creating a powerful state that stretched from the Alps to Bologna in the south.

Venice too embarked on a campaign of territorial expansion. Before the 15th century the city had tended to concentrate on building up its maritime trading empire, but now this was in danger because of the rise of the Ottoman Turks. Venice was also threatened to the west by the increasing power of Milan. In order to counter these twin threats to its wealth, Venice began to conquer neighboring cities. It soon brought a large area of northeastern Italy under its control, including the key cities of Padua, Verona, and Vicenza, which were taken in 1404 and 1405.

The aggressive political strategies of Milanese rulers such as the Visconti had also posed a threat to the city of Florence, which was still being run as a commune. In response Florence also expanded the territory under its control, seizing the port of Pisa in 1406. However, despite the emergence of large territorial states such as Venice, Milan, and Florence, some small city-states continued to thrive in the period of the Renaissance. For example, the city of Lucca, located to the northwest of Florence, managed to thwart attempts by its larger neighbor to conquer it and remained independent until the 18th century.

Above: This 15th-century painting by the artist Giovanni Toscani shows horses parading before a race in the city of Florence. Horse races were popular forms of entertainment in the Italian cities of the Renaissance.

SEE ALSO

♦ Brunelleschi
♦ Este Family
♦ Florence
♦ Genoa
♦ Gonzaga Family
♦ Government, Systems of
♦ Italy
♦ Medici Family
♦ Padua
♦ Papal States
♦ Sforza Family
♦ Venice

Classicism

The ancient civilizations of Greece and Rome are often known as the classical civilizations. Their art, architecture, philosophy, and literature were regarded by many later cultures as representing a Golden Age of human endeavor. The desire to preserve, revive, imitate, and if possible, surpass classical civilization is called classicism and lay at the heart of the European Renaissance of the 15th and 16th centuries.

The Renaissance was not the first classical revival; indeed, the heritage of Greece and Rome had never been completely lost or forgotten. The Byzantine Empire, which lasted from 474 to 1453, considered itself to be the direct heir of Greek and Roman civilization, and until its fall in 1453 the Byzantine capital, Constantinople (present-day Istanbul), was a treasure house of classical works of art and manuscripts.

In western Europe before the 15th century classical revivals were usually short-lived and limited, confined to monasteries or courts. During what is known as the Carolingian *Renovatio* (Renewal) the emperor Charlemagne (742–814) encouraged monks to study classical writings, especially those of thinkers such as Plato and Socrates.

In the Renaissance classicism was a much more secular (nonreligious) and widespread movement. By the 16th century many educated men and women across Europe were able to read

Left: A view of ruined Roman buildings in the Forum, Rome, with the Colosseum in the background. In the Renaissance architects began to study Roman ruins such as these in order to understand and emulate them in their own work.

Above: A book illustration from a 15th-century Italian edition of Virgil's Aeneid. *Demand for classical texts increased in the Renaissance, and many copies and translations were produced.*

Greek and Roman authors in the original languages and could quote them freely. Some people even christened their children with names from classical mythology, such as Hector, Achilles, and Cassandra.

CHANGING ATTITUDES

The classicism of the Renaissance also differed from earlier attitudes to antiquity (the ancient Greek and Roman world) in its desire to collect, preserve, and study its remains—which included sculptures, writings, and buildings.

In the medieval period people had had few qualms about melting down bronze statues of classical gods and goddesses or ransacking the ruins of Roman buildings for marble. By the early 15th century, however, a few people were beginning to emphasize the importance of conservation. One of the first was an Italian merchant named Cyriacus, who in 1420 compiled a classical handbook called *A Commentary on Ancient Things*.

EARLY ARCHAEOLOGY

In the following decades Cyriacus's pioneering attitude became widespread. Scholars began to collect, edit, and translate surviving texts by Greek and Roman writers. Wealthy patrons amassed collections of classical manuscripts, sculptures, gems, and other ancient artifacts.

The interest in classical antiquities was the beginning of what is today called archaeology. The first recorded excavation for classical remains took place in 1506, when Giovanni da Udine (1494–1564) dug beneath the ancient baths of Trajan in Rome and discovered a copy of the celebrated antique statue known as the *Laocoön*. Together with other excavated pieces such as the *Farnese Bull* and the *Belvedere Torso*, the *Laocoön* was put on display in the Vatican, where the classical statues were studied by Renaissance artists.

ROLE MODELS

Classical architecture, art, and literature were studied and preserved not simply for their own sake; they also provided inspiration. Renaissance architects, artists, and writers based their work on classical models, using them as yardsticks against which their own achievements could be measured.

Some poets and dramatists wrote works in Latin, closely modeled on ancient writers. Others used classical forms, themes, and stories in a more fruitful way to inspire work written in their own language. The French writer Pierre de Ronsard (1524–1585), for example, wrote poetry that was rich with classical references; he even began a national epic called *La Franciade*, which he wanted to be the French equivalent of the Roman writer Virgil's famous *Aeneid*. The English dramatist William Shakespeare (1564–1616) also drew on the plays and poetry of ancient Rome—he based *The Comedy of Errors* on a play by the Roman dramatist Plautus (about 254–184 B.C.).

Classicism was especially influential in the fields of art and architecture. In the mid-15th century Italian architects such as Leon Battista Alberti (1404–1472) revived elements of ancient Roman architecture. Alberti also wrote about classical architecture, basing his writings on the ideas of the Roman architect Vitruvius (first century B.C.), who had composed the only ancient treatise (book) on the subject to survive through to Renaissance times.

The 15th century also saw the revival of many classical art forms, including friezes, coins, portrait busts, statuettes,

---

Classicism was especially influential in the fields of art and architecture

---

and equestrian sculptures (portraits of a ruler or military leader on horseback). Artists also used classical motifs, themes, and myths in their work, although often with a Christian gloss. For example, in his painting *The Expulsion from Eden*, which shows Adam and Eve being expelled from the Garden of Eden, the Italian artist Masaccio (1401–1428) based Eve's pose on a celebrated classical sculpture called the *Capitoline Aphrodite*—Aphrodite was the Greek goddess of love.

Painters and sculptors also drew on what they perceived to be the spirit of classical art, placing a renewed emphasis on the dignity of the human body, harmonious composition, and naturalism (truth to nature).

SURPASSING THE MASTERS

Few artists or writers were content with the straightforward imitation of antiquities, however. Many felt that they could not only equal but surpass the

Greeks and Romans. The Italian sculptor Donatello (about 1386–1466) made an equestrian monument to Gattamelata (1450), a famous Venetian condottieri (mercenary soldier), which was inspired by the Roman sculpture of the Emperor Marcus Aurelius in the city of Rome. Donatello also added daring distortions to create a dynamic effect when people looked up at the sculpture on its high base. Likewise, the great artist Michelangelo (1475–1564) was famous for his work in the antique manner, although he also included distortions that make his later paintings and sculptures more powerful, weighty, and dynamic than any classical models.

Since the Renaissance classical art and civilization have continued to influence European and western cultures. Even today painters, writers, thinkers, and architects find fresh inspiration from the achievements of Greece and Rome—and often in ways that were first formulated by the innovative, creative men and women of the 15th and 16th centuries.

Below: This relief carving of a battle is an early work by Michelangelo based on his study of classical sculpture.

Clergy

The clergy are those members of a church who have been ordained—that is, officially appointed to preach the gospels and to forgive sins. In the Renaissance period the church was the greatest landowner in Europe, and the clergy were responsible for administering these lands. Members of the clergy were therefore not just priests, but also landowners and politicians.

In order to become a priest, a man had to have a good character and some education, and be at least 25 years old. Once he was ordained as a member of the clergy, he gained important privileges. Clerics could not be arrested, nor could they be tried in criminal courts. Because they were not supposed to fight, and taxes were originally a substitution for serving in a ruler's army, clerics did not have to pay taxes on their property. They could, however, freely engage in business.

THE BISHOPS

In the hierarchy of the Catholic church the most important type of clergyman was the bishop. Bishops had additional privileges and responsibilities beyond those of the simple priest. A bishop was the church's chief officer in each of the specific church regions known as dioceses. He had the power to ordain priests, as well as to assign them to parishes and to judge them in his court. In addition to their power within the church bishops were often political rulers and therefore were responsible to kings as well as to the pope.

Left: Two of the clergy's duties—confirmation (above) and baptism (below)—are shown in this stained-glass window from the 15th century.

Although the word "anticlericalism" was not used until the 19th century, it describes an attitude that was widespread during the Renaissance—a deep hatred of the clergy. In the Renaissance many people resented both the church's wealth and the dubious means by which many priests built up their riches. One cardinal reported to Pope Eugenius IV that corrupt German priests were in danger of being murdered by their own congregations.

Many critics resented the special privileges of the clergy. Others attacked the practices of simony (purchasing church offices) and pluralism (holding several church positions at the same time). Other church practices of the time were also considered by some critics to be corrupt, such as the selling of indulgences to reduce the amount of time spent in purgatory (see box).

ARCHBISHOP RAISES MONEY

In 1517 the German archbishop Albert of Brandenburg began a major campaign of selling indulgences. He was attempting to raise money to cover the huge fee demanded by the papacy in return for appointing him bishop of three different German provinces. Albert's actions soon aroused the anger of the monk and religious reformer Martin Luther (1483–1546), whose teachings led to the split between Catholicism and Protestantism.

Since the Protestant religion was born out of people's opposition to the corruption of the clergy, it is not surprising that the powers and privileges of Catholic and Protestant clergymen varied greatly. Ordained by a bishop, a Catholic priest was supposed to have special powers, such as the ability during the Mass to turn bread and water into the body and blood of Christ. A Protestant clergyman, however, was chosen by the community, rather than ordained by a bishop. He had no greater spiritual powers than any other Christian, and his primary function was simply to preach the word of God.

SEE ALSO
♦ Catholic Church
♦ Luther
♦ Protestantism
♦ Reformation

INDULGENCES

An indulgence is the cancelation of the punishment assigned for a person's sins. According to Catholic teaching, even after someone had been forgiven for a sin through the sacrament of penance, he or she still had to undergo some form of punishment. People who died without undergoing all their punishments had to do so in the afterlife, in purgatory. By granting an indulgence the church could decrease or cancel out this period of punishment.

By the Renaissance period indulgences were regularly given in exchange for simple donations of money to the church. To critics of the church it appeared that the clergy were allowing the wealthy to bribe their way directly into heaven. The practice of the selling of indulgences outraged many people, the most important being the German monk Martin Luther. The Roman Catholic church continues to grant indulgences today, although it takes care to avoid the abuses of the 16th century.

Right: A 16th-century portrait of Albert of Brandenburg, whose corrupt campaign of selling indulgences outraged Martin Luther and so sparked off the wave of protest that led to the Reformation.

Communications

Compared to today, methods of communication were slow and unreliable in the Renaissance. There were no national postal systems, and letters and packages were usually carried by merchants, who traveled regularly between countries. Urgent messages were delivered by messengers on horseback. The speed at which information traveled depended on transportation systems; roads remained little improved from medieval times, and the quickest and safest means of travel was by boat.

At the most basic level local communities communicated among themselves as they had done for centuries. To pass on warnings of danger such as invasions, they lighted fires on hills and rang bells in church and town hall towers. However, a more sophisticated system was needed to pass on detailed information. Rulers and governments required precise reports about their territories and enemies; the church needed to convey information about changes in its teachings; and bankers and merchants needed to know about new markets and exchange rates.

AMBASSADORS AND MESSENGERS

During the early Renaissance Italian towns began to station ambassadors in rival city-states and, later, in other principalities and kingdoms. Ambassadors not only represented their government's interests abroad, they also gathered intelligence about foreign communities and sent secret reports by special messenger to their home governments.

Rulers also depended on accurate information about their own kingdoms. The French king Louis XI (1423–1483) was able to weaken the power of the French nobility partly because of up-to-date information brought to him by messengers who daily scurried from one

Above: This 15th-century painting shows the arrival of English envoys (diplomatic agents) in Venice, Italy, with documents from the king. Envoys were used to carry confidential reports and secret orders, often written in code, to the rulers of foreign lands and ambassadors stationed abroad.

end of his kingdom to the other. The emperor Maximilian I also had a network of messengers, although due to the size of the Holy Roman Empire, his system was more expensive to maintain and less efficient.

SPEED AND ACCURACY

Messengers who had access to fresh mounts could cover great distances in a few days; one called Thomas della Croce is reported to have traveled on an urgent diplomatic mission from London to Milan in six days. The Catholic church operated one of the best-organized and most efficient systems of messengers called *cursores* (runners), who traveled across Europe with papal bulls (official letters from the pope). Following the Council of Florence, during which leaders of the Catholic and Orthodox churches agreed to a shortlived union, news of the achievement reached England from Italy in just two weeks.

Along with speed the accuracy of information was an important consideration. Rulers had to guard against messages falling into the wrong hands and subsequently being altered. For this reason the duchy of Milan in Italy developed sophisticated codes for its diplomatic correspondence.

BANKERS AND MERCHANTS

Like rulers and governments, bankers and merchants also required accurate information from distant lands. When businessmen involved in far-flung commercial enterprises such as the wool or spice trades knew where the demand for their goods was greatest, they gained huge competitive advantages over rivals. Bankers whose profits

Above: A colored woodcut depicting a messenger of the Renaissance period. Communications depended on messengers traveling on horseback, by boat, or on foot.

SEE ALSO

♦ Bankers and Banking
♦ Capitalism
♦ Merchants
♦ Navigation
♦ Printing
♦ Trade
♦ Transportation

partly depended on exchanging different currencies needed to know what factors influenced currency fluctuations in various places.

Free cities in Germany joined together in alliances such as the Hanseatic League and the Swabian League and established regular messenger services that were similar to modern postal systems. One of the reasons that southern German cities such as Augsburg, Nuremberg, and Ulm became important in the banking industry is that they were a part of a reliable communications system.

LINES OF COMMUNICATION

Many large banks and businesses had offices in more than one country, making international communication easier. For example, the Italian Medici and Strozzi banking families had branches in Flanders as well as Italy.

The national and international trade routes set up by these bankers and merchants also provided the main means of transporting letters and parcels. Letters were carried with shipments of goods, although it might be weeks or months before the ship left port—so they took rather longer than the swift messenger service used by rulers and the church.

A crucial advance in the spread of information and ideas during the Renaissance was the invention of printing in the middle of the 15th century. The new technology meant that books could be produced much more quickly, efficiently, and cheaply than before. Many were written in Latin, a language understood by all scholars, and bankers and merchants distributed books throughout Europe.

Condottieri

Condottieri were mercenary soldiers in the pay of Italian city-states from the mid-14th century onward. The mercenaries were named after the *condotta* (the Italian word for contract) that was drawn up by their employers to define the obligations of each party.

Mercenary soldiers are those who fight purely for pay and owe allegiance to no state or nation. They were nothing new in Europe—mercenaries had fought widely in the armies of ancient Greece. However, the conditions in Renaissance Italy, where city-states were almost continually at war with one another, made the employment of mercenary companies commonplace.

The condottieri's contracts, drawn up between the captains of their companies and the city councils or lords, were simply legal documents outlining conditions of employment. They specified in great detail the exact number of men contracted to fight, how they would be equipped and armed, where they would fight, and for how long. The employers pledged themselves to pay agreed sums for the services rendered. Most condottieri were heavily armed cavalry.

CHANGING RELATIONSHIPS

The condottieri's relationship with their employers, governed purely by financial reward, was radically different from that which existed between soldiers and their employers in the Middle Ages, when the idea of service to one's lord dominated the way armies were put together. Companies of condottieri rarely felt very much loyalty toward their employers and were notorious for changing sides if someone made them a better offer.

To the ordinary people of Italy the condottieri presented a considerable menace. During times of peace the mercenaries had little to do and no way of supporting themselves, so they would often just loot and plunder the homes of helpless civilians.

The condottieri often showed less enthusiasm for genuine battle, however. The company captains were aware that their soldiers were their only way of making money and so were reluctant to risk them in battle more than necessary. Because of this, wars involving two sets of condottieri were often relatively bloodless.

Above: Paolo Uccello painted this monument to the English condottieri leader John Hawkwood in the 15th century. Hawkwood and his men fought for various Italian city-states from 1360 onward.

SEE ALSO

♦ Arms and Armor
♦ Italy
♦ Warfare

Constantinople

The Turkish city now called Istanbul has been known by two other names in its long history. Until 330 A.D. it was called Byzantium; for the next 1,600 years it was known as Constantinople. The city officially assumed its present name in 1930. In the Middle Ages it was the heart of a great Christian empire and a major cultural center. After its capture by the Ottoman Turks in 1453 it became the capital of a powerful Muslim empire.

Byzantium was founded as a colony by the ancient Greeks in about 660 B.C. and prospered because of its position at the mouth of the Black Sea, which made it a focal point of trade between Europe and Asia. Eventually, it became part of the Roman Empire, and in 330 A.D. the emperor Constantine moved his capital there. The city's official name was New Rome, but it was soon known as Constantinople.

When the Roman Empire split in two in 395, Constantinople became the capital of the Eastern Empire. After the Western Empire collapsed in the fifth century, Constantinople was left as the world's major stronghold of Christianity and as a great beacon of western civilization—the place where the cultural traditions of Greece and Rome were upheld.

At its peak Christian Constantinople had a population of about a million and

Below: The Hagia Sophia in Constantinople. Originally built between 532 and 537 A.D. as a Christian church, it was converted into a mosque in the 15th century by the Ottoman Turks.

THE WALLS OF CONSTANTINOPLE

Constantinople was well protected by nature, since it was largely surrounded by water. It was only from the west that it could be approached by land, and there it was defended by a set of walls that had long been regarded as virtually impregnable. Originally built in the fifth century, the walls had been improved and repaired many times; parts of them are still standing.

The city's western defenses consisted of an inner wall about 35 ft (11m) high, as well as a lower outer wall, and a moat. This triple barrier stretched in an arc about 3 miles (5km) long and was extremely effective.

The great walls of Constantinople had protected the city for hundreds of years and withstood several sieges before they were finally breached in 1453 by the Ottoman Turks under Mehmed II.

The Ottoman forces bombarded the walls with a number of huge cannons, one of which was capable of delivering cannonballs that weighed 800 lb. (365kg). On the only previous occasion that the city had been captured—by the Crusaders in 1204—the walls had remained intact, since the attack was made mainly from the sea.

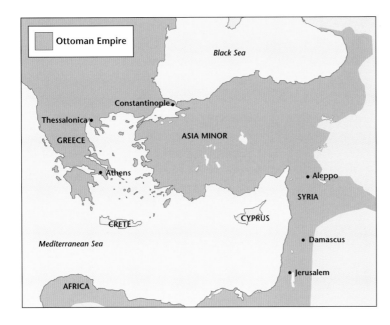

Above: The position of Constantinople, and the spread of the Ottoman Empire in the mid-16th century. Constantinople linked the east and west of the Ottoman Empire, and the main east-to-west trade route passed through it.

was a place of great wealth and magnificence, but by the 14th century the city had declined considerably. For several centuries it had come under military threat from both east and west, most importantly from the Ottoman Turks.

OTTOMAN RULE

The Ottomans had conquered much of the empire's eastern territory, and after several failed attempts their forces finally took Constantinople in 1453. The Ottomans were under the com-

mand of Mehmed II (1432–1481), who immediately set about restoring Constantinople to its former glory.

One of the first things that Mehmed did was take steps to increase the city's population, which had fallen to around 10,000 in the aftermath of the conquest. Mehmed actively encouraged people who had fled the city to come back, offering to return their goods. He also ordered his empire's provincial governors to send families to the new capital. His policies were successful, and by 1480 the city's population had increased to 100,000. Although most of these people were Muslims, a large number of Christians and Jews also lived in the city, and they were allowed to practice their religions in freedom.

NEW BUILDINGS

Much of the old city of Constantinople had been destroyed in the siege that preceded the conquest of 1453. Because of this Mehmed embarked on an extremely ambitious building program aimed at making the city a suitably magnificent capital for his empire. The Ottomans put up many splendid buildings, including mosques, palaces,

offered to attract skilled craftsmen to the city. Among the famous artists who visited Constantinople in the years following the Ottoman conquest was the Italian painter Gentile Bellini (about 1429–1507), who was sent there by the doge (or ruler) of Venice. During his stay in the city Bellini painted a famous portrait of Mehmed II.

> *Constantinople continued to be an extremely important trading center for goods such as spices and silks*

For years Constantinople had been home to Genoese and Venetian merchants who profited from the great amount of trade that passed through the city. After the city's fall to the Ottomans the Italian merchants were quick to come to friendly terms with the new rulers. Constantinople continued to be an extremely important trading center through which goods such as spices and silks passed to Europe from India and China. Despite the opposition of the Catholic church—which did not approve of dealings with Muslims—many western traders formed close ties with the Ottomans.

Constantinople continued to expand after Mehmed II's death in 1481, and a highpoint was reached in the reign of his eventual successor, Suleyman the Magnificent (ruled 1520–1566). The most spectacular building put up during Suleyman's reign was the palace built between 1525 and 1529 on the site of Mehmed's old palace, the Topkapi Saray. Visitors to Suleyman's new palace spread tales of its splendor throughout Europe, greatly increasing the prestige of the Ottoman sultan.

and a grand bazaar, or covered market, that remains in use to this day. However, the most famous mosque from this period, the Hagia Sophia (Holy Wisdom), was converted by the Ottomans from an ancient Christian church. The mosque still survives in good condition, and its huge dome is regarded as one of the masterpieces in the history of world architecture.

ART AND TRADE

Constantinople's reputation as a center for art, built up during its Christian era, continued after the Ottoman conquest. A number of special concessions were

Above: The seige of Constantinople by the Ottoman Turks, depicted in an illustration from a 15th-century book.

SEE ALSO

♦ Genoa
♦ Otttoman Empire
♦ Trade
♦ Venice

Timeline

♦ **1305** Giotto begins work on frescoes for the Arena Chapel, Padua—he is often considered the father of Renaissance art.

♦ **1321** Dante publishes the *Divine Comedy*, which has a great influence on later writers.

♦ **1327** Petrarch begins writing the sonnets known as the *Canzoniere*.

♦ **1337** The start of the Hundred Years' War between England and France.

♦ **1353** Boccaccio writes the *Decameron*, an influential collection of 100 short stories.

♦ **1368** The Ming dynasty comes to power in China.

♦ **1377** Pope Gregory XI moves the papacy back to Rome from Avignon, where it has been based since 1309.

♦ **1378** The Great Schism begins: two popes, Urban VI and Clement VII, both lay claim to the papacy.

♦ **1378** English theologian John Wycliffe criticizes the practices of the Roman Catholic church.

♦ **1380** Ivan I of Muscovy defeats the army of the Mongol Golden Horde at the battle of Kulikovo.

♦ **1389** The Ottomans defeat the Serbs at the battle of Kosovo, beginning a new phase of Ottoman expansion.

♦ **1397** Sigismund of Hungary is defeated by the Ottoman Turks at the battle of Nicopolis.

♦ **1397** Queen Margaret of Denmark unites Denmark, Sweden, and Norway under the Union of Kalmar.

♦ **1398** The Mongol leader Tamerlane invades India.

♦ **1399** Henry Bolingbroke becomes Henry IV of England.

♦ **1400** English writer Geoffrey Chaucer dies, leaving his *Canterbury Tales* unfinished.

♦ **1403** In Italy the sculptor Ghiberti wins a competition to design a new set of bronze doors for Florence Cathedral.

♦ **c.1402** The Bohemian preacher Jan Hus begins to attack the corruption of the church.

♦ **1405** The Chinese admiral Cheng Ho commands the first of seven expeditions to the Indian Ocean and East Africa.

♦ **1415** Jan Hus is summoned to the Council of Constance and condemned to death.

♦ **1415** Henry V leads the English to victory against the French at the battle of Agincourt.

♦ **c.1415** Florentine sculptor Donatello produces his sculpture *Saint George*.

♦ **1416** Venice defeats the Ottoman fleet at the battle of Gallipoli, but does not check the Ottoman advance.

♦ **1417** The Council of Constance elects Martin V pope, ending the Great Schism.

♦ **1418** Brunelleschi designs the dome of Florence Cathedral.

♦ **1420** Pope Martin V returns the papacy to Rome, bringing peace and order to the city.

♦ **c.1420** Prince Henry of Portugal founds a school of navigation at Sagres, beginning a great age of Portuguese exploration.

♦ **1422** Charles VI of France dies, leaving his throne to the English king Henry VI. Charles VI's son also claims the throne.

♦ **c.1425** Florentine artist Masaccio paints the *Holy Trinity*, the first painting to use the new science of perspective.

♦ **1429** Joan of Arc leads the French to victory at Orléans; Charles VII is crowned king of France in Reims Cathedral.

♦ **1431** The English burn Joan of Arc at the stake for heresy.

♦ **1433** Sigismund of Luxembourg becomes Holy Roman emperor.

♦ **1434** Cosimo de Medici comes to power in Florence.

♦ **1434** The Flemish artist Jan van Eyck paints the *Arnolfini Marriage* using the newly developed medium of oil paint.

♦ **1439** The Council of Florence proclaims the reunion of the Western and Orthodox churches.

♦ **c.1440** Donatello completes his statue of David—the first life-size bronze sculpture since antiquity.

♦ **1443** Federigo da Montefeltro becomes ruler of Urbino.

♦ **1447** The Milanese people declare their city a republic.

♦ **1450** The condottiere Francesco Sforza seizes control of Milan.

♦ **1450** Fra Angelico paints *The Annunciation* for the monastery of San Marco in Florence.

♦ **1453** Constantinople, capital of the Byzantine Empire, falls to the Ottomans and becomes the capital of the Muslim Empire.

♦ **1453** The French defeat the English at the battle of Castillon, ending the Hundred Years' War.

♦ **1454–1456** Venice, Milan, Florence, Naples, and the papacy form the Italian League to maintain peace in Italy.

♦ **1455** The start of the Wars of the Roses between the Houses of York and Lancaster in England.

♦ **c.1455** The German Johannes Gutenberg develops the first printing press using movable type.

♦ **1456** The Florentine painter Uccello begins work on the *Battle of San Romano*.

♦ **1461** The House of York wins the Wars of the Roses; Edward IV becomes king of England.

♦ **1461** Sonni Ali becomes king of the Songhai Empire in Africa.

♦ **1462** Marsilio Ficino founds the Platonic Academy of Florence— the birthplace of Renaissance Neoplatonism.

♦ **1463** War breaks out between Venice and the Ottoman Empire.

♦ **1465** The Italian painter Mantegna begins work on the Camera degli Sposi in Mantua.

♦ **1467** Civil war breaks out in Japan, lasting for over a century.

♦ **1469** Lorenzo the Magnificent, grandson of Cosimo de Medici, comes to power in Florence.

♦ **1469** The marriage of Isabella I of Castile and Ferdinand V of Aragon unites the two kingdoms.

♦ **1470** The Florentine sculptor Verrocchio completes his *David.*

♦ **1476** William Caxton establishes the first English printing press at Westminster, near London.

♦ **1477** Pope Sixtus IV begins building the Sistine Chapel.

♦ **c.1477** Florentine painter Sandro Botticelli paints the *Primavera*, one of the first large-scale mythological paintings of the Renaissance.

♦ **1478** The Spanish Inquisition is founded in Spain.

♦ **1480** The Ottoman fleet destroys the port of Otranto in south Italy.

♦ **1485** Henry Tudor becomes Henry VII of England—the start of the Tudor dynasty.

♦ **1486** *The Witches' Hammer* is published, a handbook on how to hunt down witches.

♦ **1488** Portuguese navigator Bartholomeu Dias reaches the Cape of Good Hope.

♦ **1491** Missionaries convert King Nzina Nkowu of the Congo to Christianity.

♦ **1492** The Spanish monarchs conquer Granada, the last Moorish territory in Spain.

♦ **1492** Christopher Columbus lands in the Bahamas, claiming the territory for Spain.

♦ **1492** Henry VII of England renounces all English claims to the French throne.

♦ **1493** The Hapsburg Maximilian becomes Holy Roman emperor.

♦ **1494** Charles VIII of France invades Italy, beginning four decades of Italian wars.

♦ **1494** In Italy Savonarola comes to power in Florence.

♦ **1494** The Treaty of Tordesillas divides the non-Christian world between Spain and Portugal.

♦ **1495** Leonardo da Vinci begins work on *The Last Supper* .

♦ **1495** Spain forms a Holy League with the Holy Roman emperor and expels the French from Naples.

♦ **1498** Portuguese navigator Vasco da Gama reaches Calicut, India.

♦ **1498** German artist Dürer creates the *Apocalypse* woodcuts.

♦ **1500** Portuguese navigator Pedro Cabral discovers Brazil.

♦ **c.1500–1510** Dutch painter Hieronymus Bosch paints *The Garden of Earthly Delights.*

♦ **c.1502** Italian architect Donato Bramante designs the Tempietto Church in Rome.

♦ **1503** Leonardo da Vinci begins painting the *Mona Lisa.*

♦ **1504** Michelangelo finishes his statue of David, widely seen as a symbol of Florence.

♦ **c.1505** Venetian artist Giorgione paints *The Tempest.*

♦ **1506** The Italian architect Donato Bramante begins work on rebuilding Saint Peter's, Rome.

♦ **1508** Michelangelo begins work on the ceiling of the Sistine Chapel in the Vatican.

♦ **1509** Henry VIII ascends the throne of England.

♦ **1509** The League of Cambrai defeats Venice at the battle of Agnadello.

♦ **1510–1511** Raphael paints *The School of Athens* in the Vatican.

♦ **1511** The French are defeated at the battle of Ravenna in Italy and are forced to retreat over the Alps.

♦ **1513** Giovanni de Medici becomes Pope Leo X.

♦ **1515** Thomas Wolsey becomes lord chancellor of England.

♦ **1515** Francis I becomes king of France. He invades Italy and captures Milan.

♦ **c.1515** German artist Grünewald paints the *Isenheim Altarpiece*.

♦ **1516** Charles, grandson of the emperor Maximilian I, inherits the Spanish throne as Charles I.

♦ **1516** Thomas More publishes his political satire *Utopia*.

♦ **1516** Dutch humanist Erasmus publishes a more accurate version of the Greek New Testament.

♦ **1517** Martin Luther pins his 95 theses on the door of the castle church in Wittenburg.

♦ **1519** Charles I of Spain becomes Holy Roman emperor Charles V.

♦ **1519–1521** Hernán Cortés conquers Mexico for Spain.

♦ **1520** Henry VIII of England and Francis I of France meet at the Field of the Cloth of Gold to sign a treaty of friendship.

♦ **1520** Portuguese navigator Ferdinand Magellan discovers a route to the Indies around the tip of South America.

♦ **1520** Süleyman the Magnificent becomes ruler of the Ottoman Empire, which now dominates the eastern Mediterranean.

♦ **1520–1523** Titian paints *Bacchus and Ariadne* for Alfonso d'Este.

♦ **1521** Pope Leo X excommuicates Martin Luther.

♦ **1521** The emperor Charles V attacks France, beginning a long period of European war.

♦ **1522** Ferdinand Magellan's ship the *Victoria* is the first to sail around the world.

♦ **1523–1525** Huldrych Zwingli sets up a Protestant church at Zurich in Switzerland.

♦ **1525** In Germany the Peasants' Revolt is crushed, and its leader, Thomas Münzer, is executed.

♦ **1525** The emperor Charles V defeats the French at the battle of Pavia and takes Francis I prisoner.

♦ **1525** William Tyndale translates the New Testament into English.

♦ **1526** The Ottoman Süleyman the Magnificent defeats Hungary at the battle of Mohács.

♦ **1526** Muslim Mongol leader Babur invades northern India and establishes the Mogul Empire.

♦ **c.1526** The Italian artist Correggio paints the *Assumption of the Virgin* in Parma Cathedral.

♦ **1527** Charles V's armies overrun Italy and sack Rome.

♦ **1527–1530** Gustavus I founds a Lutheran state church in Sweden.

♦ **1528** Italian poet and humanist Baldassare Castiglione publishes *The Courtier*.

♦ **1529** The Ottoman Süleyman the Magnificent lays siege to Vienna, but eventually retreats.

♦ **1530** The Catholic church issues the "Confutation," attacking Luther and Protestantism.

♦ **1531** The Protestant princes of Germany form the Schmalkaldic League.

♦ **1531–1532** Francisco Pizarro conquers Peru for Spain.

♦ **1532** Machiavelli's *The Prince* is published after his death.

♦ **1533** Henry VIII of England rejects the authority of the pope and marries Anne Boleyn.

♦ **1533** Anabaptists take over the city of Münster in Germany.

♦ **1533** Christian III of Denmark founds the Lutheran church of Denmark.

♦ **1534** Paul III becomes pope and encourages the growth of new religious orders such as the Jesuits.

♦ **1534** Luther publishes his German translation of the Bible.

♦ **1534** The Act of Supremacy declares Henry VIII supreme head of the Church of England.

♦ **c.1535** Parmigianino paints the mannerist masterpiece *Madonna of the Long Neck*.

♦ **1535–1536** The Swiss city of Geneva becomes Protestant and expels the Catholic clergy.

♦ **1536** Calvin publishes *Institutes of the Christian Religion*, which sets out his idea of predestination.

♦ **1536** Pope Paul III sets up a reform commission to examine the state of the Catholic church.

♦ **1537** Hans Holbein is appointed court painter to Henry VIII of England.

♦ **1539** Italian painter Bronzino begins working for Cosimo de Medici the Younger in Florence.

♦ **1539** Ignatius de Loyola founds the Society of Jesus (the Jesuits).

♦ **1541** John Calvin sets up a model Christian city in Geneva.

♦ **1543** Andreas Vesalius publishes *On the Structure of the Human Body*, a handbook of anatomy based on dissections.

♦ **1543** Polish astronomer Copernicus's *On the Revolutions of the Heavenly Spheres* proposes a sun-centered universe.

♦ **1544** Charles V and Francis I of France sign the Truce of Crespy.

♦ **1545** Pope Paul III organizes the Council of Trent to counter the threat of Protestantism.

♦ **1545** Spanish explorers find huge deposits of silver in the Andes Mountains of Peru.

♦ **1547** Charles V defeats the Protestant Schmalkaldic League at the Battle of Mühlberg.

♦ **1547** Ivan IV "the Terrible" declares himself czar of Russia.

♦ **1548** Titian paints the equestrian portrait *Charles V after the Battle of Mühlberg*.

♦ **1548** Tintoretto paints *Saint Mark Rescuing the Slave*.

♦ **1550** Italian Georgio Vasari publishes his *Lives of the Artists*.

♦ **1553** Mary I of England restores the Catholic church.

♦ **1554** Work begins on the Cathedral of Saint Basil in Red Square, Moscow.

♦ **1555** At the Peace of Augsburg Charles V allows the German princes to determine their subjects' religion.

♦ **1556** Ivan IV defeats the last Mongol khanates. Muscovy now dominates the Volga region.

♦ **1556** Philip II becomes king of Spain.

♦ **1559** Elizabeth I of England restores the Protestant church.

♦ **1562** The Wars of Religion break out in France.

♦ **1565** Flemish artist Pieter Bruegel the Elder paints *Hunters in the Snow*.

♦ **1565** Italian architect Palladio designs the Villa Rotunda, near Vicenza.

♦ **1566** The Dutch revolt against the Spanish over the loss of political and religious freedoms:

Philip II of Spain sends 10,000 troops under the duke of Alba to suppress the revolt.

♦ **1569** Flemish cartographer Mercator produces a world map using a new projection.

♦ **1571** Philip II of Spain and an allied European force defeat the Ottomans at the battle of Lepanto.

♦ **1572** In Paris, France, a Catholic mob murders thousands of Huguenots in the Saint Bartholomew's Day Massacre.

♦ **1572** Danish astronomer Tycho Brahe sees a new star.

♦ **1573** Venetian artist Veronese paints the *Feast of the House of Levi*.

♦ **1579** The seven northern provinces of the Netherlands form the Union of Utrecht.

♦ **1580** Giambologna creates his mannerist masterpiece *Flying Mercury*.

♦ **1585** Henry III of France bans Protestantism in France; civil war breaks out again in the War of the Three Henrys.

♦ **1586** El Greco, a Greek artist active in Spain, paints the *Burial of Count Orgaz*.

♦ **1587** Mary, Queen of Scots, is executed by Elizabeth I of England.

♦ **c.1587** Nicholas Hilliard paints the miniature *Young Man among Roses*.

♦ **1588** Philip II of Spain launches his great Armada against England —but the fleet is destroyed.

♦ **1589** Henry of Navarre becomes king of France as Henry IV.

♦ **1592–1594** Tintoretto paints *The Last Supper*.

♦ **1596** Edmund Spencer publishes the *Faerie Queene*, glorifying Elizabeth I as "Gloriana."

♦ **1598** Henry IV of France grants Huguenots and Catholics equal political rights.

♦ **1598** In England the Globe Theater is built on London's south bank; it stages many of Shakespeare's plays.

♦ **1600–1601** Caravaggio paints *The Crucifixion of Saint Peter*, an early masterpiece of baroque art.

♦ **1603** Elizabeth I of England dies and is succeeded by James I, son of Mary, Queen of Scots.

♦ **1610** Galileo's *The Starry Messenger* supports the sun-centered model of the universe.

♦ **1620** The Italian painter Artemisia Gentileschi paints *Judith and Holofernes*.

Glossary

A.D. The letters A.D. stand for the Latin Anno Domini, which means "in the year of our Lord." Dates with these letters written after them are measured forward from the year Christ was born.

Altarpiece A painting or sculpture placed behind an altar in a church.

Apprentice Someone legally bound to a craftsman for a number of years in order to learn a craft.

Baptistery Part of a church, or a separate building, where people are baptized.

B.C. Short for "Before Christ." Dates with these letters after them are measured backward from the year of Christ's birth.

Bureaucracy A system of government that relies on a body of officials and usually involves much paperwork and many regulations.

Cardinal An official of the Catholic church, highest in rank below the pope. The cardinals elect the pope.

Classical A term used to describe the civilizations of ancient Greece and Rome, and any later art and architecture based on ancient Greek and Roman examples.

Colonnade A row of columns supporting an arched or a flat structure.

Condottiere A mercenary soldier, that is, a soldier who will fight for any employer in return for money.

Contemporary Someone or something that lives or exists at the same period of time.

Diet A general assembly of representatives of the Holy Roman Empire.

Distaff A stick with a cleft end used to hold the raw wool or flax from which the thread is drawn when spinning by hand.

Envoy Someone who is sent abroad to represent the government.

Excommunicate To ban someone from taking part in the rites of the church.

Flemish A word used to describe someone or something from Flanders, a region including present-day Belgium and parts of the Netherlands and France.

Fresco A type of painting that is usually used for decorating walls and ceilings in which pigments (colors) are painted into wet plaster.

Frieze A horizontal band around the top of a building decorated with sculpture or other ornamentation.

Genre A term used to describe paintings depicting scenes from daily life.

Hanseatic League A trading association of towns around the Baltic Sea that was set up in the late 13th century. It flourished between the 14th and 16th centuries.

Heresy A belief that is contrary to the accepted teachings of the church.

Heretic Someone whose beliefs contradict those of the church.

Humanism A new way of thinking about human life that characterized the Renaissance. It was based on the study of "humanities"— that is, ancient Greek and Roman texts, history, and philosophy—and stressed the importance of developing rounded, cultured people.

Hundred Years' War A long-drawn-out war between France and England, lasting from 1337 to 1453. It consisted of a series of campaigns with periods of tense peace in between.

Indulgences Cancelations of punishment for sins. Indulgences were often granted by the church in return for money.

Laity or lay people Anyone who is not of the clergy.

Mason A builder, particularly one skilled in working in stone.

Motif A repeated element in a design.

Orders A term used in classical architecture for the five different types of classical columns and the rules governing their use.

Patron Someone who orders and pays for a work of art.

Patronage The act of ordering and paying for a work of art.

Pediment In classical architecture the triangular-shaped structure at the top of a building façade (front); also the moldings above windows and doorways.

Perspective A technique that allows artists to create the impression of three-dimensional space in their pictures. Near objects appear larger, and far objects are shown as smaller.

Piecework Work that is paid for according to the amount done (rather than according to the time it has taken).

Pilaster An architectural feature consisting of a vertical strip that sticks out slightly from a wall like a flattened column.

Pluralism Holding two or more offices (positions). Members of the clergy often held more than one post, which meant they could not perform their duties properly in all of them.

Portico A term used in classical architecture to describe a roofed structure with columns and a pediment (see above) on the front of a building; also known as a temple front.

Prose The ordinary form of written language—that is, not poetry.

Sarcophagus A stone coffin, often decorated with carved panels.

Simony Buying or selling a church office.

Theologian Someone who studies religious faith, practice, and experience.

Triptych A picture or carving consisting of three panels side by side. It was often used as an altarpiece.

Vatican The headquarters of the pope and papal government in Rome.

Vernacular The language of the ordinary people, rather than Latin.

Further Reading

Bouwsma, William James. *John Calvin: A Sixteenth-Century Portrait.* Oxford: Oxford University Press, 1989.

Branley, Franklyn Mansfield. *Keeping Time: From the Beginning and into the 21st Century.* Boston, MA: Houghton Mifflin, 1993.

Brown, Patricia Fortini. *Art and Life in Renaissance Venice.* New York: Harry N. Abrams, 1997.

Brucker, Gene A. *Florence: The Golden Age 1138–1737.* Berkeley, CA: University of California Press, 1998.

Bruschi, Arnaldo. *Bramante.* London: Thames & Hudson, 1977.

Cecchi, Alessandro. *Agnolo Bronzino.* Florence, Italy: Scala, 1996.

Cervantes Saavedra, Miguel de. *Don Quixote de la Mancha.* Oxford: Oxford University Press, 1998.

Chaucer, Geoffrey. *The Canterbury Tales* (translated into modern English by Nevill Coghill). New York: Penguin USA, 2000.

Chaucer, Geoffrey (editor Larry D. Benson). *The Riverside Chaucer.* Boston, MA: Houghton Mifflin, 1987.

Cotterell, Arthur. *Eyewitness: Ancient China.* New York: DK Publishing, 2000.

Crankshaw, Edward. *The Habsburgs: Portrait of a Dynasty.* New York: Viking Press, 1971.

Day, Nancy. *Your Travel Guide to Renaissance Europe.* Minneapolis, MN: Runestone Press, 2001.

Duffy, Eamon. *Saints and Sinners: A History of the Popes.* New Haven, CT: Yale University Press, 1999.

Gartner, Peter. *Brunelleschi.* Cologne, Germany: Könemann, 1998.

Gibson, Walter S. *Hieronymus Bosch.* London: Thames & Hudson, 1985.

Goldberg, Jake. *Miguel De Cervantes.* Broomall, PA: Chelsea House Publishing, 1993.

Grant, R.G. *Capitalism.* Austin, TX: Raintree/Steck Vaughn, 2001.

Hand, John Oliver, et al. *The Age of Brueghel: Netherlandish Drawings in the Sixteenth Century.* Cambridge, UK: Cambridge University Press, 1987.

Hersey, George L. *High Renaissance Art in St. Peter's and the Vatican: An Interpretive Guide.* Chicago, IL: University of Chicago Press, 1993.

Howarth, Sarah. *Renaissance People.* Brookfield, CT: Millbrook Press, 1992.

Huang, Ray. *1587: A Year of No Significance.* New Haven, CT: Yale University Press, 1986.

Jestaz, Bertrand. *Architecture of the Renaissance: From Brunelleschi to Palladio.* New York: Harry N. Abrams, 1996.

Kapr, Albert. *Johann Gutenberg: The Man and His Invention.* Brookfield, VT: Scholar Press, 1996.

King, Ross. *Brunelleschi's Dome: How a Renaissance Genius Reinvented Architecture.* New York: Walker, 2000.

Kinross, Lord. *Ottoman Centuries: The Rise and Fall of the Turkish Empire.* New York: William Morrow, 1977.

Koldeweij, Jos, Paul Vandenbroeck, and Bernard Vermet. *Hieronymus Bosch: The Complete Paintings and Drawings.* New York: Henry N. Abrams, 2001.

Levathes, Louise. *When China Ruled the Seas: The Treasure Fleet of the Dragon Throne, 1405–1433.* New York: Simon & Schuster, 1994.

Lubkin, Gregory. *A Renaissance Court: Milan under Galeazzo Maria Sforza.* Berkeley, CA: University of California Press, 1994.

MacDonald, Fiona. *A 16th Century Mosque.* New York: Peter Bedrick Books, 1994.

Mallett, Michael Edward. *Mercenaries and Their Masters: Warfare in Renaissance Italy.* London: Bodley Head, 1974.

Martens, Maximiliaan P.J. *Bruges and the Renaissance: Memling to Pourbus.* New York: Harry N. Abrams, 1999.

McGrath, Alister E. *A Life of John Calvin: A Study in Shaping of Western Culture.* Oxford: Blackwell Publishers, 1993.

Millar, John Fitzhugh. *Classical Architecture in Renaissance Europe, 1419–1585.* Williamsburg, VA: Thirteen Colonies Press, 1987.

Morley, Jacqueline. *A Renaissance Town.* New York: Peter Bedrick Books, 1996.

Necipoglu, Gulru. *Architecture, Ceremonial, and Power: The Topkapi Palace in the Fifteenth and Sixteenth Centuries.* Cambridge, MA: MIT Press, 1992.

Norman, Diana. *Siena and the Virgin: Art and Politics in a Late Medieval City State.* New Haven, CT: Yale University Press, 1999.

O'Reilly, Wenda Brewster. *The Renaissance Art Book: Discover Thirty Glorious Masterpieces by Leonardo da Vinci, Michelangelo, Raphael, Fra Angelico, Botticelli.* Palo Alto, CA: Birdcage Books, 2001.

Pilliod, Elizabeth. *Pontormo, Bronzino, and Allori: A Genealogy of Florentine Art.* New Haven, CT: Yale University Press, 2001.

Rady, Martyn C. *The Emperor Charles V.* New York: Longman, 1988.

Santi, Bruno. *Botticelli.* Florence, Italy: Scala, 1994.

Scalini, Mario. *Benvenuto Cellini.* Florence, Italy: Scala, 1995.

Sterckx, Pierre. *Bruegel: A Gift for Telling Stories.* Broomall, PA: Chelsea House Publishing, 1995.

Trease, Geoffrey. *The Condottieri: Soldiers of Fortune.* New York: Holt, Rinehart & Winston, 1971.

Willard, Charity Cannon. *Christine de Pizan: Her Life and Works.* New York: Persea Books, 1984.

Wills, Gary. *Venice, Lion City.* New York: Simon & Schuster, 2001.

Websites

World history site
www.historyworld.net

BBC Online: History
www.bbc.co.uk/history

The Webmuseum's tour of the Renaissance
www.oir.ucf.edu/wm/paint/glo/renaissance/

Virtual time travel tour of the Renaissance
library.thinkquest.org/3588/Renaissance/

The Renaissance
www.learner.org/exhibits/renaissance

National Gallery of Art—tour of 16th-century Italian paintings
www.nga.gov/collection/gallery/ita16.htm

Uffizi Art Gallery, Florence
musa.uffizi.firenze.it/welcomeE.html

Database of Renaissance artists
www.artcyclopedia.com/index.html

Set Index

MAPS
The maps in this book show the locations of cities, states, and empires of the
Renaissance period. However, for the sake of clarity, present-day place names are
often used.